Rambles in the Black Forest

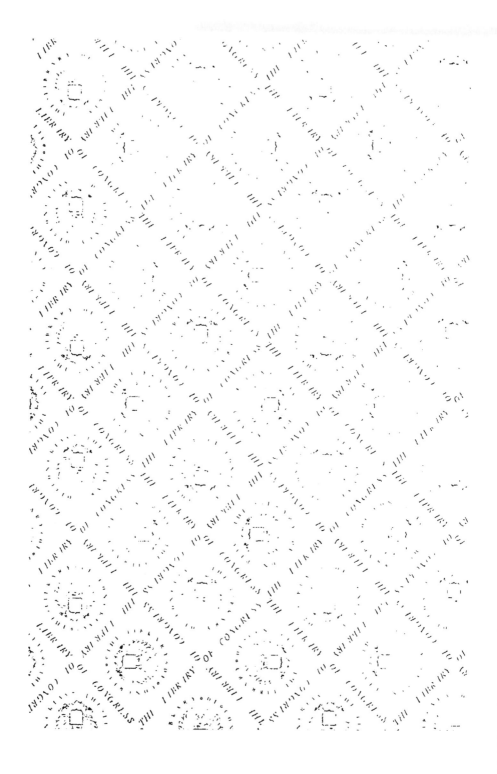

RAMBLES IN THE BLACK FOREST

RAMBLES IN THE BLACK FOREST

RAMBLES IN THE BLACK FOREST

BY

I. A. R. WYLIE

AUTHOR OF "MY GERMAN YEAR"
"DIVIDING WATERS" "THE RAJAH'S PEOPLE"

WITH 3 ILLUSTRATIONS BY C. LIEBICH, 3 BY G. ENGLISH
AND 22 FROM PHOTOGRAPHS

BOSTON
DANA ESTES & COMPANY

Published 1911

Copyright in the British Empire by Mills & Boon Limited, London
Printed by Morrison & Gibb Limited, Edinburgh

124

CONTENTS

v

LIST OF ILLUSTRATIONS

———◆———

IN COLOUR

THE PICTURE ON THE COVER SHOWS THE RUINS
OF HERRENALB, WITH THE PINE TREE GROW-
ING FROM THE TOP OF THE ARCHWAY.

IN MONOTONE

LIST OF ILLUSTRATIONS

RAMBLES IN
THE BLACK FOREST

CHAPTER I

A PRELIMINARY RAMBLE

I HAVE chosen the title to this little book only after much doubt and many twinges of conscience, fearing to mislead my readers by the term 'rambles,' which in a usual way infers something altogether pedestrian. But, indeed, where in the English language is a word to be found which comprehends every mode of locomotion except flying? How compose a title which will immediately call up before the mind's eye a vivid picture of the author on foot, of the author on a bicycle, of the author in a puffing and snorting little motor-car belonging to a past generation of motor-cars, of the author in a comfortable if

A   I

hired victoria—we must not boast—of the author, last, but not least, wearied and broken-spirited, in a common ox-wagon, having been picked up ten miles from anywhere by a pitying village yokel? The obvious answer is the word 'tour,' but to my mind the title *Tours Through the Black Forest* would be even more misleading—in fact, positively deceitful. It might persuade some prospective holiday-maker to buy the book under the impression that it is a kind of guide and friend through all the intricacies of the German time-table, a saving help in those times of doubt and un-certainty when twenty hopeful porters, repre-senting as many 'first-class hotels,' await his final choice. He might imagine carefully mapped excursions—one day here, two days there, half an hour for this waterfall, and so on, with all the overblown signposts righted and pointing in the truthful direction for his benefit. All this he might imagine, and be greatly deceived, for I have no wish to enter into any competition with great firms of 'Globe-Trotting Mentors.' If I had the wish I should have no claim to be heard, and those who trusted me would soon find themselves bitterly disappointed. I merely wish to describe the Black Forest as I know and love it, and I have chosen the word 'rambles' because, for

2

me, it expresses something unrestrained, haphazard, something altogether unbound by laws and miles. It suggests an easy jog-trot which will give you time, if it so pleases you, to lie full length in the grass and dream yourself away amongst the pine-tops, or to stop and study the flowers which grow in such rich profusion along the roadside, or to watch the wild deer grazing in the cool shadows, or to listen to the roar of the torrent as it thunders on its way valley-wards. Whatever else happens, you will at least not be hurried, and if you are tired after a long walk, and a peasant's cart comes your way and you are offered a lift, there will be no tiresome pedant to chide you that it would be incorrect to accept, since you are a professed pedestrian; on the contrary, you will be told that it is the only sensible thing to do, and that nobody but the confirmed mile-eater, as the Germans picturesquely call him, cares for plodding on when he is already hot and weary. In a word, this book is for the rambler, as I understand him, not for the tourist, who is a very different person. The genuine tourist never rambles, he tours, and therein lies the fundamental and all-important difference. The world is full of tourists; some of them are rich and laden with much belabelled boxes, some of them

3

are poor—you meet them on the dusty high-roads, burdened with heavy knapsacks, hatless, coatless, with red, hot faces, which they lift a moment in order to contemplate you lying in the shade of the trees. As a rule they see nothing of the country through which they are trudging. Their eyes are fixed on the dust, and the only point of interest for them is the encouraging mile-stone which is bringing them nearer to their destination.

Rich and poor, all these people are 'touring,' and the tourist has only one object in life— to 'do' something, to 'get' somewhere, and to have the right to say he has 'done it,' or 'got there' all on foot, or all in a motor-car, or all in a first-class sleeping compartment, just as his particular ambition tends. And, rich and poor, all these people are more or less mad— at any rate, pitiful self-deceivers. They call 'pleasure' what is in reality a strenuous hustle and bustle which no one really enjoys; they call 'sight-seeing' a blind race to some given point which has no further interest for them from the moment that they have reached it.

Such people only learn to know the country they travel through from the exterior, and they never learn to love it. They may be able to catalogue every picture in the galleries and every 'notable' sight, but they will never learn

4

to know the 'genius' of the places they see. They are rather like those other people who pride themselves on having what they call 'an eye for faces,' but who have never learnt to study an expression, much less to penetrate below the surface to the character or emotion in which that expression has its source. Such folk judge entirely by outward appearances, and consequently they rarely love and they rarely praise with genuine feeling. They are impressed by a beautiful face or by a gorgeous apparel, but, after all, neither the one nor the other can form objects of lasting affection.

So also the tourist—only such countries impress him which have something stupendous to show; if he is rich and luxurious he likes grand scenery and grand hotels, if he is of the mile-eating type he likes to climb famous mountains and famous passes, and in both cases a purely pastoral beauty, the charm of a peaceful landscape, has no hold upon him. In his eyes one valley, one low, fir-covered mountain looks like another, and he groans after the obvious magnificence of a Mont Blanc.

I make these observations, not out of ill-feeling against a harmless enough section of my fellow-creatures, or because I have any selfish interest in the well-doing of Black Forest hotel-keepers, but simply in the endeavour to explain the marked neglect with which the Black Forest is treated by foreigners. In the summer you may meet trains full of English, American, French, and Russian travellers, bound for the Alps, for that already overcrowded Switzerland : but from the moment you leave the plains behind you, and wander up into the Forest, which lies at the east of the grand route, you find yourself almost entirely amongst the native Germans. For them the Black Forest is a legitimate playground, a spot of earth created to suit their temperament and their taste.

There are few grand hotels—the average German's pet abomination—and the scenery is essentially Teutonic—if I may coin the expression—that is to say, poetic and lovely, romantic and wild, but neither cold nor tremendous, and only rendered awe-inspiring by the spirit of past ages which broods over its solitudes.

Therefore, wherever you go you will meet Germans of every class and from every corner of the Empire, but perhaps one Englishman in a hundred. Him you may greet as a sort of Masonic brother, since only a genuine love and understanding has driven him aside out of the excited, heated stream of holiday-makers bound for Europe's so-called playground

A PRELIMINARY RAMBLE

I have been told, of course, that Switzerland offers far more attraction, that the hotels are better, that the scenery is grander; that, on the other hand, the Black Forest is monotonous and consequently depressing. *Bien entendu* it was a tourist who offered me this explanation—a rambler would have known better.

He who has really travelled through the Black Forest with his eyes and heart open, will tell you that not only can it stand comparison with Switzerland, but that it is incomparable. It is true there are no white-capped mountains, no glaciers, no dangerous passes; the stupendous, awe-inspiring properties of the Alps are, in a word, wholly absent; but, indeed, in these forms of beauty the Black Forest makes no attempt to enter into competition. One might almost say that she disdains the more boastful splendours of her neighbour, standing alone and unique in her own quieter grandeur, and calling with an irresistible eloquence to those who understand her language. Not every one understands her language. I have no doubt that there are hundreds of travellers who stand awestruck before a Swiss mountain, and who will never recognise the impressiveness of a Black Forest gorge. The heights and depths are not great enough for them. They prefer something which crushes

7

the senses beneath a weight of magnificence, something which requires no effort to understand and appreciate. The Black Forest lover—and she has only one kind of lover, the ardent admirer who admits no rival—must have the love of nature implanted in him, he must be himself something of a poet, and something of a musician, and something of an artist, even though he never composed a sonnet, or a song, or painted a landscape. He must be able to see in every valley, in every waterfall, in every mountain a subtle distinction, a delicate character which lends each a separate personality, a charm unlike all others. His observant eyes must be able to mark the changes which come with a marvellous swiftness over the landscape—the wonderful colours which reveal themselves amongst what seems to the careless tourist a monotonous olive. In the loneliness he must be able to see life—the hundred forms of beautiful and strange life which move noiselessly in the shadows—and in the silence hear the music of the fir trees and the drowsy hum of a countless hoard of unseen workers.

It seems a great deal to expect of a simple and unpretentious rambler, but, indeed, without these virtues of heart and mind the Black Forest must remain a closed book for him. She makes no vulgar appeal to the senses;

like every one worth knowing she holds herself back in reserve until she feels the true understanding of a sympathetic personality.

For the Black Forest has her own personality—so much so that I must fain allow her a personal pronoun—and like that of her inhabitants it is so profound, so unique, that it has withstood the levelling atmosphere of the globe-trotter and remained itself, sphinx-like, for those who give themselves neither the time nor the trouble to learn to understand, a tireless teacher for those who come with heart and eyes open to receive her lessons.

Therefore I warn the great army of mere sight-seers, of bustling tourists, and society-loving folk to leave her untroubled. They will find nothing to attract them, and will only go away disgusted with the dreariness and monotony of a much over-rated district.

But the rambler will understand and love her. It may be that he will have to learn, for some ramblers are born and some ramblers are made; some ramblers see from the beginning, and some have to be taught to see. The present writer humbly confesses to belonging to the latter group. There was indeed a time when I greatly preferred the more brilliant effects of the Alps, and found the Black Forest, as I then knew it, a rather monotonous health resort.

RAMBLES IN THE BLACK FOREST

The truth was that I had never done anything but tour through the country. I had stopped at the big hotels and been hustled and bustled about in the most busy season and in the midst of a thorough holiday crowd. I had done the correct excursions and seen the correct sights, but I had remained, nevertheless, blind and deaf to the real character, the real meaning of that which I saw and heard. Afterwards I learnt to know people who had made their home in one of the quiet valleys, who lived there through summer and winter, and they slowly opened my eyes and ears. They took me among the village folk and up into the mountains, where the tourist foot never wanders; to peasants' huts hidden away up in the heights; they told me of the folk-lore, the people's customs, the legends which haunt the mountains, and gradually the Black Forest became imbued with a spirit, a living personality whose language I had learnt a little to understand. Let me confess at once that my understanding is far from complete—I think it is a confession which even the greatest authorities must make. For Nature has given us in the Black Forest an inexhaustible expression of herself, and whereas elsewhere, as in Switzerland, she holds aloof, a stern, cold goddess who locks her secrets and her wisdom in an impenetrable bosom amongst

A BLACK FOREST CLOCK-MAKER.

the low, pine-covered mountains, she relaxes her
stern features and becomes the living companion
of those who have learnt to love her. And
whether you are a born rambler or only in the
making, it is worth while to learn to love this
nature, this Spirit of the Black Forest, as we
will call her. Then when you stand on what
seems to you the highest summits and gaze
over the sweep of mountains which stretch away
like a purple haze into the sunset, you will not
complain of a want of grandeur. You will
realise that you are standing at the heart of
Nature herself, that she has opened her gates
wide to you, and that the world which lies
before you has been her undivided kingdom
from all eternity. You will not complain of
an oppressive quiet, for you will have learnt
to understand the voice of the Forest which
will tell you legends and strange tales from
a history which stretches right back to the
beginning of man. And you will not complain
of loneliness, for, as I have said, you will have
learnt to see life in the seeming solitude, and
your imagination will have learnt to conjure up
the quaint earth men and all the fairy spirits
which still live there for the punishment of
the wicked and the reward of the virtuous.
And as you stand there a change will come over
you : no cold, glacial peak rises above you to

remind you of your own insignificance; the
world lies beneath you, a wonderful forest-world
whose beauty seems to elevate you above yourself, to fill you with an idealism which perforce
forsakes you in the stifling lowlands, and in
the crowd and strife of the cities. You feel no
arrogance. The world beneath you is not less
than you. Nor do you feel oppressed, crushed
beneath the menace of a Nature who stands
before you as an eternal enemy, asking life for
every daring encroachment upon her territory.
Here Nature claims you as a very part of herself.
All that is best, noblest, grandest in her finds
an echo in all that is best, noblest, and grandest
in your own heart. She calls awake slumbering
melodies and half-forgotten dreams, and the
breeze which she sends to you over the pines
sweeps away the mists, the unhealthy vapours
of modern life, and brings, for the moment at
least, an absolute quiet and peace. Peace,
health, mental and physical, such are the gifts
which the Spirit of the Black Forest gives to
the heart- and mind-wearied humanity who year
after year come to her saving power for help.

It is not without reason that sanitoria for
every form of suffering are to be found dotted
amidst the solitude. In the solemn, elevating
grandeur of her mountains, in the quiet gaiety
of her valleys, in the healing peace of her

forests, in the pure air, heavy with the perfumes of the pines, mind and body can rest, can draw health and gather strength to renew the battle which had overpowered them. But in case it be suspected that I have shares with Dame Nature in this favoured 'health resort' which she has erected, I will say no more for the present. Suffice that it is to the true rambler, the nature lover, the man or woman seeking vigour and relaxation, that these rambles are dedicated.

There are hundreds of rambles which I have left undescribed, for they would fill almost as many volumes, but if I have encouraged the reader to seek them out I have attained my humble object. At any rate, this chapter has, I hope, justified my own claim to the title of a 'rambler.'

CHAPTER II

WHICH VENTURES TO BE MILDLY INSTRUCTIVE

THE rambler need not be alarmed by the above title. I have no intention of belabouring him with scientific facts, or burdening him with a heavy supply of geographical, zoological, botanical, and geological wisdom. Science, and even an over-supply of wisdom, are not for the average rambler, who likes to go haphazard, and wants to enjoy nature without having to bother about the whys and wherefores of his enjoyment. I know, from my own experience, that there are some well-meaning but objectionable people who during a stroll will never leave you in peace, but are always engaged in cataloguing the different trees and plants, and worrying you about the possible and impossible geological make-up of that particular district. All this is very unnecessary and very disturbing. It does not much matter to the Black Forest rambler whether the ground he walks on is

14

composed of granite or sandstone; what does matter to him is that his path is shady and beautifully kept, and that the flowers growing on either side offer him a delight entirely independent of names and distinctions. And even if the rambler be a man of science whose chief enjoyment in life is the gleaning of fresh knowledge, he will at least be wise enough not to look for a detailed scientific exposition of the various points of interest in a book which professes to deal purely and simply _with rambles. He will know that each branch of science would require a volume to itself, and if he wants that volume it is easy enough to obtain.

Nevertheless, I feel impelled to touch lightly on certain features, because, in the first place, they may encourage the student to seek further; in the second, because they are directly connected with that intangible but very real being whom I have ventured, for want of a better term, to christen the Spirit of the Black Forest. For example, the rambler who is ignorant of the country's wild, romantic history, will miss something of the magic which haunts the old ruins whose shattered walls frown over the valleys. He will feel himself less drawn towards the inhabitants, in whose veins flow the proud Roman and Celtic blood; the grandeur of the mountains will impress him less, since their origin is unknown to him.

For there was a time when they were not mountains, when the peaceful valleys over which he gazes had no existence. How long ago the gigantic changes took place none can say, but it is certain that no human eye witnessed them.

A hundred thousand years back — a few thousand this way or that is of no importance— a broad tableland spread from the present-day Bohemia to the present-day France. In the first instance it was composed chiefly of granite, but, as the ages passed, the waters brought with them a mighty and increasing sediment of rock and stone which rose above the original bed to a height of about three thousand feet. By a natural process the gases and burning lava lying beneath in the heart of the tableland cooled, bringing with them a contraction, a shrinkage of the earth which left immense cavities beneath the surface. On this frail crust lay the whole burden, which eventually proved too heavy. The crust yielded, the terrific masses thundered down into the depths, leaving behind solitary standing points which we now call mountains, and forming beneath valleys of very varying lengths and characters. The Black Forest was one of the definite results.

As we know it to-day, it extends from Karlsruhe south as far as Basel, a distance of about one hundred and seventy-five kilometres, and from east to west its breadth varies from thirty-five kilometres (in the north) to seventy-five kilometres (in the south). Full three-quarters of this valuable territory lie in the Grand Duchy of Baden, a quarter only in Wurtemberg. The geographical divisions in the Black Forest are so sharply and clearly defined that the rambler who is fond of mapping out distinct districts which he intends to explore has a comparatively easy task before him. He need only take the valleys and follow them up to their head, and see all that the Black Forest has to show in pastoral and wild romantic beauty.

And here these valleys can be divided into two distinct groups. Far the greater number run from east to west, and are accompanied by a stream or river which pours down from the heights into the Rhine, and from which the valley takes its name. From west to east, that is to say, on the western slope of the high ridge of mountains running northwards, the valleys are fewer and usually of a wilder character. Their rivers flow into the Donau, which, as all the world knows, takes its source at Donaueschingen ; but I fancy it must sometimes puzzle an undecided rivulet as to which of the two great rivers it shall honour with its humble addition, since the frontier between the eastern and western slope is of the narrowest.

These two groups of valleys can be divided again into smaller groups, which repeat themselves with slight though distinctive variations throughout the Black Forest. Some, such as the Gutach, are purely pasture land. Fresh green meadows stretch on either side up to the low mountains which lie well back from the quietly flowing river. There is a broad outlook and from a slight eminence one can look away over the villages clustering on the banks of the great Rhine plain beyond.

These valleys lay no claim to romantic grandeur, but they have a charm which is all their own, and as characteristic of the Black Forest as any wild and rocky cleft. It is here that the rambler finds the picturesque villages, and the wealthy, conservative old peasants who cling to their customs and their dress with a pertinacity which, alas ! is yielding to the inroads of 'modern fashion.' But we will come back to these interesting folk later when our rambles lead us past their homesteads.

In contrast to these valleys there are the narrow gorges whose rocky walls, rising sheer up on either hand, allow scarce room for more than the bed of the torrent which rushes tumultuously towards the plain. There are others which broaden out gradually, others which retain a certain breadth throughout, and each, though it can always be reckoned as belonging to a certain class, has a certain characteristic either in respect of its scenery or its inhabitants, which the rambler grows gradually to recognise and to appreciate. These also we shall visit later on; for the present we must leave them for the mountains themselves.

As I have warned the reader at the beginning, there are no snow-peaked Alps here to catch the eye of the jaded, sight-seeing tourist. The highest mountain, the Feldberg, rises only to about 4500 feet, and though in past ages it was covered with snow throughout the year, all traces of winter now disappear at the beginning of June and even earlier. Nevertheless, on a suitable day—a very rare day, it might be remarked—the view from the summit is a magnificent one: the Rhine lies beneath, and over all the neighbouring mountains the Feldberg is undisputed monarch.

To the south-west lie its two most important rivals, the Blauen and the Belchen, both over 4000 feet; northwards the Kandel rises well above its neighbours, but from thence the mountains gradually sink, and only here and there, as in the case of the Hornisgrinde and the Kniebis, can they boast of more than 3000 feet of grandeur. 'Grandeur' in connection with such small elevations may seem absurd to the climber of Alpine peaks, but, indeed, actual measurements go for little in the Black Forest.

Wherever you are you always seem to have the world beneath you, and this is specially true of the northern parts which, according to feet and inches, should be considerably less imposing than the south, but which, on the contrary, have regions of unrivalled beauty. I have no doubt there are any number of travellers who would rise in protest against this statement, but it is, after all, only a matter of taste, and I confess to a weakness for the north, and to having found the south somewhat over-estimated by comparison.

One of the many reasons given for the so-called 'monotony' of the Black Forest is the 'absence of water.' I put the statement in inverted commas because it is not my statement, and I only repeat it because it has so often been repeated to me. Were the charge true, I admit that it would be a very grave one, but I venture to protest against it. It is true there are few lakes of any great importance; the Titisee and the Schluchsee make the greatest claim to attention, though there are others, such as the Feldsee, whose inferiority in size is atoned for by wilder, more romantic, surroundings. But the rivers, the torrents, the rivulets which stream down every hill and mountain-side— and the waterfalls! The rambler who fails to find the waterfall at every stopping-place must, indeed, be a unique individual. There are water-falls everywhere of all sorts and sizes, from the grand Triberger, whose imposing beauty has been spoilt by too much artistic cultivation on the part of over-zealous *hôteliers* with an eye to the tourist taste, to that of Allerheiligen, to my mind more natural and therefore superior. It is always a mistake when mankind imagines he can improve nature by mowing the grass, planting regular flower-beds, and turning on an artificial moonlight of various colours in a thunderstorm. A rambler who knows the Black Forest will sympathise with this sentiment.

One word more before leaving the geographical province. Throughout the country which we are about to explore the roads and paths are magnificently kept : the paths are like those of a park ; the roads make the rambler who has neglected to bring his bicycle gnash his teeth with vexation. A great deal of this advantage is owing to the nature of the soil, and to the fact that many districts are closed to the motorists ; but a great deal more is owing to the praiseworthy efforts of the Black Forest Association (Schwarzwald Verein), who keep up the paths, erect signposts, and act as the rambler's guardian angel throughout.

In speaking of the various means of transit, mention must be made of the railway—naturally the work of the Government, and one of which it has every reason to be proud. 'The Schwarzwald Bahn' is, in fact, one of the 'sights' and rivals some of the greatest Swiss engineering feats. Though the greater number of health resorts lie some miles from the actual station, still there is no spot in the Black Forest which the railway does not make perfectly accessible, and for this blessing one must offer up humble thanks to the Government. No private company would ever have built it, for it neither pays nor is it of much strategical use, being incapable of transporting great loads. It is a great piece of enterprise, out of which the traveller certainly takes the profit.

Another 'last word' must be devoted to the weather. The weather ! If one could only find a 'last word' for it in these erratic days ! It is with fear and trembling that I make the following statements, for which I refuse to hold myself in any way responsible. Settled weather, either for good or bad, is rare in the Black

Forest. The morning can be cloudless, there
may be a terrific thunderstorm in the afternoon,
and a glorious sunset in the evening. One day
may be tropical, another may find you huddled
up against the welcome stove with blue fingers,
and wondering why you did not bring your
winter things with you. All this does not
sound very hopeful, but I must add that the
climate is nevertheless a healthy one in summer
and in winter. There are at least no fogs;
whilst below in the valleys less fortunate mortals
are making their way through mist and mud,
the Black Foresters are enjoying a clear air and
a dry soil; for no matter how much it has
rained, the roads and paths are always irre-
proachable. A south-west wind predominates,
and thunderstorms which first break against the
sides of the Blauen and then roll from mountain
to mountain northwards are anything but
rarities. They are a part of the Black Forest,
an expression of her spirit, adding to her
majesty, and the rambler who has not heard
the artillery of a hundred armies roaring about
his ears has missed the chance of listening to
her in her grandest moods.

The temperature, as I have hinted, varies with
every day, and also, naturally enough, with the
altitude. On the whole one can say that the
lower resorts are too hot for July and August,

but delightful for June and September; but everywhere the nights are cool and refreshing, and nowhere has one to suffer from the dried-up vegetation and dusty, stifling atmosphere which so often spoil the holidays in other parts of the world. The Black Forest knows no high summer in the general sense of the term. The trees bear always a fresh green until they change for their autumn tints; the meadows are always verdant; the vegetation seems to be always that of early summer. As a rambler who knows the Black Forest in spring, in summer, in autumn, and in winter, I can recommend each season, though always with due regard to the places chosen.

For the winter the highest points are not too high. The cold is dry and keen but not too intense; and the wonderful forest-world clothed in spotless white, adorned with glittering gems whose facets flash in the cold sunshine, with pine and fir burdened with frozen snow, clean-cut against a sky of Italian blue, should be something of a revelation even to the most spoilt rambler, and even though he knew nothing of the noble art of ski-ing.

For spring the choice must be a cautious one, but if the lower roads are chosen it is fully worth while to run the risk which the weather offers. The first pale green of the re-awakening birks

THE BLACK FORESTER'S HOME IN WINTER.

and beeches creeping up among the solemn olive of the unchanging forest firs and pines reveal to the rambler the very embodiment of Spring herself. To my thinking there is only one season more beautiful in the Black Forest, and that the autumn, when Nature lavishes her whole wealth of colour to perfect the fiery magnificence of her own apotheosis. But it must be admitted that the rambler who ventures up into the heights in either of these two seasons must be of the hardier sort, prepared for minor hardships, and capable of making up for the lack of exterior warmth by vigorous exercise. Moreover there are, as everywhere, periods when the Black Forest is wholly unenjoyable. Roughly speaking, the rambler may hope for sufficiently fine weather up to the end of September, when, though the autumnal beauty is at its height, the cold becomes unpleasantly noticeable and the chief hotels close.

December marks the opening of the winter season in the higher resorts, which lasts until about February. From February until the middle of April the climate is cold, damp, and most uninviting, but from that time onwards the rambler may make his plans. For the ordinary holiday-maker who is less anxious for physical exertion and more desirous of basking in warm sunshine, I venture to recommend the middle of June to the middle of July, and the end of August to the beginning of September. At both times the country is in its best summer mood; the hotels are cheaper and not so over-crowded, and the weather in an average year (I wonder what an average year nowadays is really like!) fairly settled.

So much for geographical and climatic information! I might well ramble on and become botanical and zoological in my in-structiveness, but I refrain, leaving such things to the dim future. Only I should be doing the Black Forest an injustice, I should be depriving her of one of her most powerful appeals to the imagination, if I allowed her history to pass unnoticed, and therefore a brief survey, which leaves volumes of romance untold, may be here acceptable.

CHAPTER III

THE FIRST BLACK FOREST RAMBLERS

THE dark recesses of the Black Forest have indeed seen much history and many changes, both, for the most part, of a violent character. Of those changes the average traveller would suspect little on his rambles, for each change has brought with it the destruction of the last, each race of men has destroyed the traces of its predecessor. And so the Black Forest, in spite of her past, in spite of her stubborn inhabitants, who have fought for their existence in the most unfruitful fastnesses, in spite of the thousand-headed troup of tourists, in spite of railways, has retained something of her virginity, of her old jungle-darkness and solitude.

History has left few traces, and yet the history of the Black Forest dates as far back and is as stormy and bloody as that of any country in Europe.

Of her first inhabitants, the Celts, little is known save that they were a people on the first steps of civilisation. A few stone implements and utensils found in the most prosperous valleys testify to their one-time existence, though it appears that they never ventured up into the forest darkness, then inhabited by hunger-driven wolves and bears. The Celts passed, or rather became absorbed by their Roman conquerors. Under the latter's absolute sovereignty the whole character of the Black Forest changed : it became the centre of a civilisation hitherto unknown and almost unthinkable in the bleak, sparsely habited regions. The new colonists cleared their way up on to the mountain heights, built high-roads along the summits and on the jagged rocks overlooking the valleys, erected watch-towers and fortresses against the northern enemy. Thus for a time after the tumult of conquest a certain idyllic peace settled upon the forest. Not only civilisation, but imported splendour came with the Roman Conquest. The baths, as at Baden-Baden and at Badenweiler, indicate an almost unparalleled luxury, and throughout the country wheresoever the Roman foot trod sprang up small towns and villages, built after the national fashion of the builders.

Thus two centuries passed before Rome's power waned, and the first uneasy stirrings of the Germanic tribes upon the borders of the

Empire became a definite revolt. For a time
the Legions held their ground with varying
fortune, and then, like the rush of a tide, long
held in abeyance by a weakening dam, a
horde of barbarians flooded over the field of
their labours, sweeping out of existence or
demolishing almost beyond recognition every
trace of the old civilisation. Thus of the
Roman period in the Black Forest history little
remains, and that little lies in ruins. Here and
there on some solitary height the wanderer will
come across a broken, shapeless wall, and in
Badenweiler the marble baths have been spared
sufficiently to give an idea at least of their past
splendour, but the greater part of the Roman
work and the Roman civilisation has disappeared.
Once more the jungle grew over their high-
roads; their watch-towers and the hostelries
which they had built for the shelter of travellers
fell into decay. The new conquerors, wearied
of the roughness of their own climes, kept to the
valleys, and the mountains became once more
the habitation of the wolves. Yet below the
surface the Roman influence remained. Those
of the old inhabitants, a mixed Celtic-Roman
race, who had been left, carried on their own
civilisation, and slowly, insidiously, Franken
and Alemanen and such others of the Germanic
race as had made their home in and about the

Rhine valley came under the influence of those they had conquered. All this concerns us and our rambles only in so far that we shall meet the Roman influence, not in architecture or in laws or customs, but amongst the people themselves. For just as there are villages where the Huns have left a distinct trace both in names and in physical types, so there are whole districts where the traveller — especially the traveller who knows his Italy well — will find the 'Roman face' constantly reproduced amongst the peasantry. Thanks to a rigid system of inter-marriage, the latter have succeeded in remaining a race apart: physically, bearing strong traces of their ancient origin ; in character, taking after their surroundings— hardy, reserved against impertinent intrusion, honest, simple, and yet possessed of a certain rugged grandeur. But to return to their forefathers and the first of those who made the mountains their home.

After the Germanic invasion the Black Forest knew no change of masters save in times of war, when alternately she was captured and re-captured ; her barbaric conquerors retained their hard-won territory, and gradually in their turn became civilised. Christianity came amongst them, heralded for the most part by Irish monks, who founded a great number of the

monasteries which to-day mark the most popular
resorts. Pursued and persecuted by their future
converts, these monks sought refuge in the
mountains, fearing the jungle and its wolf
inhabitants less than the human inhabitants of
the valleys, and succeeded in winning a scanty
means of existence from the rocky soil. They
were, indeed, the pioneers of the Black Forest.
They opened out regions which since the Roman
days had been regarded as impregnable, and
chose the sites for their monasteries with a
wonderful forethought and a wonderful per-
ception of the beautiful. To-day the existence
of an old ruined cloister is sufficient testimony
that the surroundings are idyllic, peaceful, and
lovely, and it is hard for us ramblers of to-day
to realise what we owe to these first hardy and
daring explorers. For it followed, as a natural
consequence, that not only did they bring with
them an increasing civilisation, but the land
about them became cultivated, and little by
little their dwellings became the centre of small
but growing colonies. Converts from the
valleys, encouraged by the monks' success, and
at last hunters, wood-cutters, shepherds, and
peasants, followed their example and sought a
new existence in the depths of the mountains.
Each colonist chose out his own piece of land,
and worked on it unaided save by the members

of his family, and thence sprung a system of life which exists to-day. The modern rambler will often be struck by the solitary farms which dot the mountain-sides at wide distances from each other, and if he inquires further he will find that each farm is a world in itself, an independent kingdom ruled over by some old peasant who neither needs nor asks assistance of his neighbours. In the past, only one danger succeeded in bringing these lonely folk together, and that was a danger from a third class of pioneer. The nobility amongst the tribes of that day was at first merely the distinction between the serfs and the freemen, but later the more powerful amongst the latter adorned themselves with titles (Freiherren, Junker), and arrogated to themselves unlimited authority over those directly beneath them. Power begets rivalry, and with the rising of the self-made lords there grew up an increasing unrest. They themselves were not safe from each other, and to obtain security from attack they turned to that part of the country which offered them a natural protection. On the crags, where the old Romans had built their watch-towers—sometimes on their very ruins—these knights erected the strongholds whose broken walls we shall meet on our rambles. Thus protected and almost unassailable they turned their attention to an increase of

their wealth, and soon no peasant, no travelling
merchant, was safe from attack. Perched upon
the heights overlooking the valleys these light-
fingered nobles were able to watch the richly
laden caravans on their way northwards, and
like so many vultures swept down on the
harmless and defenceless travellers, plundered
them of their merchandise, and were back in
their strongholds before their victims could so
much as think of obtaining help, still less
revenge. Naturally the peasants suffered most,
and suffered from two quarters, since not only
were they the obvious prey for their unscrupulous
superiors, but the clergy, who had long ago
given up the frugal, hardy ways of their forerunners, exerted their spiritual and material
power over their flock to the point of tyranny.
Driven to exasperation, the peasants formed
secret leagues, and at last, in 1524, broke into a
terrible revolt. As is usual, it was a comparatively light incident which fanned the smouldering bonfire to flame.

A certain countess of Lupfen ordered her
servants to leave their harvest work in order
to gather snail-shells for her, and this last
insulting injury was the signal for an outbreak
which spread like a prairie fire over the whole
country, destroying half the monasteries and
castles, and breaking for ever the power of

both nobility and clergy. From that moment the peasants obtained their freedom, and a certain prosperity seemed likely to be the reward of their struggle, when the wars of religion broke over their head.

The Reformation had made its way through the Black Forest, starting from Switzerland, and gaining power as the nobility accepted the new teaching. It is regrettable to note, however, that the popular confession of faith veered round every time a duke or prince changed *his* mind, so that generations passed before either side could definitely claim its followers.

And meanwhile the wars did their work, calling the male population to arms, leaving the villages desolate, the fields unattended, and sending back year after year a horde of ragged vagabonds to complete the destruction of an already half-starved population. Whole villages disappeared beneath the hands of these new robbers; women and children fled to the most lonely mountain recesses, there to face a miserable death either from hunger or the fangs of the wolves, whose numbers had doubled during the time of general desolation. The hard-won civilisation and prosperity of a few years was swept away. The few castles and strongholds which the Peasants' War had left standing were reduced to ruins. The Thirty

Years' War, with religion for its watchword, had done its work. And still the Black Forest's stormy history must go on.

Under Louis XIV. and XV. of France the War of Succession once more brought war and bloodshed over the country. The wars of the Republic flooded the Black Forest with French and Austrian soldiery. Scarcely a valley or a pass that did not echo the thunder of desperate fighting, in which the peasants bore their heroic part. As most desperate of all must be noted the retreat of the French army under General Moreau through the Höllenthal. Amidst pouring rain, threatened by flooded rivers and torrents, their road blocked by Austrian troops, the Frenchmen fought their way over the mountain heights and at last reached Freiburg, a ragged, broken remnant. This struggle, the most remarkable that the Black Forest had seen, since the most remote valleys and highest summits were not spared, marks the close of her warlike history. In 1806 Napoleon I. created the Grand Duchy of Baden, which compassed three-quarters of the Black Forest. This possession remained in the same hands, the Grand Duke uniting himself to the allies after the battle of Leipzig. And thus the Forest's varying fortunes end in a noneventful history, which betokens peace and progress. And thus also ends my instructiveness and a brief survey of the past as the scene of our future rambles has witnessed it. It may happen that every here and there some moss-grown ruin, some sleeping village, will bring that past back to us, and paint for us a corner out of the great picture. At any rate, the canvas is stretched, and the genuine rambles may begin at last.

CHAPTER IV

THE SOUTH-EASTERN GATE: SINGEN AND THE HEGAU

I SUPPOSE there is scarcely a guide-book written on the subject of the Black Forest which does not take either Pfortzheim or Karlsruhe for its starting-point. I hope, therefore, that it was not a mere spirit of contrariness which led my German friend and me to start our grand summer exploration in direct opposition to all law and order. I hope there was method in our madness, or, at any rate, sufficient method, for an over-abundance of that commodity suggests the tourist rather than the rambler. It is true, that for the English traveller coming from England, Karlsruhe offers itself as the nearest entrance, and if he have but little time to spare he will do well to read this book backwards and begin, as the guide-books have it, 'at the beginning.' But if he have a few weeks before him and the desire to learn to know the Black Forest at its heart, I suggest that he follow our procedure.   There is, indeed, something vaguely disappointing for the newcomer in the all too popular resorts which lie about Karlsruhe and Baden-Baden.   The tracks are too beaten, and he has not learnt to know the Spirit of the Forest sufficiently well to overlook what is banal, overrun, and 'tripperish,' and see beyond too the inner beauty and meaning of the surroundings.   English people who take Wildbad and Hundseck for their headquarters more often than not come away with a tale of disappointment.   They have seen nothing of the peasant life, and do not believe there is anything to see. They tell you that the picturesque cottages of which they had read are either imaginary or belong to past ages, and their general impression is that of a series of rather dull, rather comfortless health resorts.   Naturally, they do not seek farther, and the real Black Forest remains unknown to them.   Had they started with the less frequented regions they would have come north possessed with understanding, and the very real—I might almost say unrivalled—beauty of such places as Allerheiligen would be revealed to them shorn of the disadvantages which its too great accessibility brings with it.

The northern Black Forest is, in fact, at once too typical and not typical enough.   Its very

A CORNER IN A BLACK FOREST COTTAGE.

beauty leads the inexperienced to believe that it is all that the Black Forest has to show, and that beauty is for him too monotonous, too obviously intended to attract the tripper eye. The romance is lacking, and all that which lends character to a country, the people and their homes, has almost entirely disappeared. I confess at once that already, before we started on our travels, we were a little weary of that which lay at our door, and that fact may have helped us to our decision. Be it as it may, whether, as I believe, with reason or simply out of the desire to get out of the beaten track, we took direct train to Constance, to the very south-east corner of the Black Forest; in other words, we defied every guide-book that was ever written. Had it not been that our somewhat vague plans commanded us to 'move on' we should probably have gone no farther, for Constance is one of the many charming towns which Baden may boast of, and the Insel Hotel a dwelling-place which offers its guests at once romance and comfort. In past generations a large Dominican monastery, it has still retained its pleasant cloisters; what was then a solemn vaulted chapel is now a stately dining-hall. The waters of the lake over which it looks flow round its walls, and cut it off by a narrow moat from the noisy streets, thus justifying its name, and lending it a certain atmosphere of dignified aloofness from the modern world, whose demands for comfort and luxury it has been compelled to satisfy. As we sat over the excellent table d'hôte dinner in the dignified loneliness of belated travellers, I could not but wonder what the shades of the old fathers were thinking of our delicacies and of the solemn attendants at our backs. Undoubtedly they were there— one felt them loitering dismally in the shadows —but whether they watched us with righteous disapproval, with envy, or with the kindly understanding of fat non-Lenten days, I do not know. Certain alone is that they neither took away our appetites nor spoilt our rest, well earned as it was. The charm which pervades the Insel Hotel pervades all Constance. History lurks in the old-world corners ; cardinals and bishops, emperors and kings, passed by in the grand pageant which the Consilium and the grey walls of once dreaded prisons call up before the imagination. And with all that solemnity from a great past there is a certain gaiety, a certain spirit of smiling and peaceful content. One is tempted to bask away one's time in pleasant idleness, allowing the fascination of the Middle Ages to alternate with the delights of to-day ; spending the cool of the afternoons on the waters which carry one out to the idyllic island of the Mainau, where the Grand Duke of Baden has his summer residence, and the evenings on the terrace overlooking the lake with its hundred reflected lights and many shadows.

In the height of the summer, mosquitoes, with a wholly reprehensible interest for newcomers, mar the pleasure of these occupations, and this disadvantage, together with the heat, should encourage travellers to choose an early month for their visit—the middle of June for preference. But Constance is the gate of the Black Forest, not the Black Forest itself, and regretfully we consigned ourselves and our belongings to the railway to be transported farther. Our road led us past a second lake—Untersee—which is in reality only a division of its superior neighbour. From the shores we caught a glimpse of the island of Reichenau with its many holy and unholy memories, for the ruined monastery which lies peacefully amidst fruitful fields and pastures does not, unfortunately, bear witness to an exemplary past. Founded, so it is said, somewhere in the year 724 by a certain Pirmin of pious memory, it soon occupied much the position of a modern fashionable church, and was patronised by all the best people of that day. Unfortunately this popularity, together with the unexampled preciousness of its relics—

the bones of St. Mark numbered among others—appears to have turned the heads of its abbots, who fell into ways of the wildest luxury. Nor was luxury the only crime attributed to them : the ruined castle, built probably by some Roman predecessor, and used by the abbots as their dwelling-place, was reduced to ruins by the lake fishers as the punishment for a peculiarly brutal act. Some of their number having ventured to ply their trade in the waters which the monastery chose to consider as private property, the abbot had them seized, and blinded them with his own hands Embittered by this unwarranted cruelty, their comrades banded together, and the broken walls of the once luxurious castle bear testimony to their revenge.

Thus we left Reichenau behind us and stopped for a few moments' breathing-space at the old historical town of Radolfzell. History dates its foundation to the seventh century, when a certain Bishop Radolf of Verona, on the search for the 'simple life,' with the permission of the abbot at Reichenau, built himself a cell and chapel on the borders of the lake. His extreme holiness attracted other pilgrims, and gradually, after his death had, as it were, sanctified the place, Radolfzell grew from a spot of religious retirement to a prosperous fishing village, and from a fishing village to the peaceful,

old-world town as it stands to-day. For us its
chief claim to interest lies in the fact that the
great poet and novelist of South Germany,
Joseph Victor von Scheffel, had his home
there, and there probably gathered together the
romance of the region, which we were to visit,
making out of vague legend a brilliant historical picture of the past. Of him and of
his work we may speak later when we reach the
places which he has made more memorable than
their memories have done.

In the meantime our train had steamed out
of the station and we had other things to think
of, namely, the fading afternoon light had
warned us that time had not stopped on our
account, and that our chances of reaching our
destination that day were becoming distinctly
problematic. My German friend thereupon
took a sympathetic train conductor into her
confidence, and, with the assistance of a much
bethumbed time-table, discovered that if we
really wished to reach Boll we should have to
travel till midnight, with the pleasant interruption of changing trains at nearly every small
station *en route*. This prospect was too much
even for our energy, and at the next stopping-
place we turned out with bag and baggage to consider the difficulty at our leisure. The difficulty
was not diminished by the fact that the platform

was entirely devoid of human life. Thus we stood there in the midst of our goods and chattels, realising for the first time how very wrong it is to break the Sabbath by travelling, and wondering if anybody in the sleepy little town was awake. And presently, just as despair was about to take hold on us, lo and behold! a figure came running full pelt in our direction, dragging on a coat as it ran, an hotel porter's cap stuck awry over a very red face. Our unexpected rescuer proved to be the man-of-all-work at the neighbouring Hotel Sonne, and he immediately appointed himself our guide and friend. Boll he had only heard of in a vague way, but he calculated it was inaccessible that night unless we went by motor-car. The idea of a motor-car was as surprising as it was agreeable. But a motor-car in connection with the dreamy little half-town, half-village in which we had landed seemed altogether out of place, and we ventured to doubt the possibility. Our guide was decided and a little hurt. Certainly there was a motor-car—there was THE motor-car in fact, though he was less sure as to whether he could obtain its services so late on Sunday evening. Would it not be wiser to stay the night and go on the following morning? Singen was, after all, a most interesting town. We looked about us. A little above the town, on a slight eminence,

44

we saw what appeared to be a well-preserved castle, built in the style of the Middle Ages, and beyond that a mountain, which rose like a solitary jagged tooth out of the undulating plain. There seemed, indeed, to be enough to occupy us for one evening at least, and yielding to the wiles of our new friend, and the pleadings of a very hungry inner man, we wended our way to the Hotel Sonne, whose windows had seemed to be watching us during our moments of hesitancy with wide-open interest.

Half-inn, half-hotel, our new lodging-place accommodated us with a pleasant bedroom and a good meal, but as there was no sitting-room, save one that was filled with a gay, beer-drinking Sunday crowd, we soon found ourselves once more on the wander. My German friend, who has a passion for old castles haunted with romance, insisted on a visit to the promising-looking erection which had at first attracted our attention, and thither, therefore, we repaired as fast as our bump of locality could guide us. The streets in the interior of the little town showed a decidedly more lively appearance than we had expected. On the so-called market-place a merry-go-round was keeping up a cheerful and wholly friendly musical contest with the solemn organ tones from a neighbouring Catholic church, where the more sober members of the community were paying their Sunday devotions. Youth, however, appeared to prefer the merry-go-round, and we had some difficulty in making our way across into the unfrequented street which led out of the town towards our destination. Our destination, however, when once reached was well worth the trouble, as we at once decided. It was a ruin that was not a ruin, for, though bearing the rough imprint of time and weather, it had still retained all the essentials of roof and covered towers, and its débris was in the last degree decorative.

"What a wonderful artist Nature is!" my German friend exclaimed, with true Teutonic enthusiasm. "See how beautifully she has toned the colouring on the walls, and look how the moss has grown in the crevices about the windows! It is really one of the most perfect examples of Middle Age architecture."

"Please, do you want to go over the theatre?" said a small voice at our elbow.

"What?" we demanded of the bare-headed, bare-footed, and not very intelligent-looking country maiden who had apparently sprung from nowhere.

"What?"

"The theatre," she repeated placidly. "Fifty pfennig entrance, please."

THE SOUTH-EASTERN GATE

We stared about us. There was nothing that looked like a theatre in sight.

"What theatre do you mean? Where?"

"There!"

Slowly the veil fell from our eyes. There was, indeed, something suspiciously picturesque about the vividly green patches of moss, and the window — yes, on closer inspection the ghastly suspicion confirmed itself—the window was a painted fraud! My German friend turned slowly and sadly away, but my feelings having been less harrowed I stayed a moment to probe deeper into the matter. It appeared that our marvel of 'Middle Age architecture' had been erected somewhere about the year 1905 A.D., and was there solely for bi-annual performances of the dramas connected with the history of the neighbourhood—in fact, a kind of worldly Oberammergau. Certainly the building was a wonderful deception, and inside and out it kept up appearances to a degree which must make the actual performances peculiarly impressive. Still, it was a bitter disappointment, and though my German friend tried to comfort herself with the reflection that the presence of a theatre of such dimensions and originality in a town that could only be called town by courtesy, proved the profound artistic and poetic—not to mention enterprising—qualities of the German people, her belief in things general was at least temporarily shaken. As a counter-irritant, therefore, I suggested that we should spend the last hour of daylight in climbing the mountain immediately before us. There was something so real about that hour's climb that I fancy my friend's sense of unreality of things had decreased before we reached the summit, and she was quite prepared to take the ruins on trust. History at least vouches for them and the broken walls; the fallen towers and turrets, in part overgrown with shrubs, indicate a troubled past; in truth, the Hohentwiel, as this lonely rock is called, has seen many changes and vicissitudes. Rising abruptly out of the gently undulating plain it formed a natural place of defence, and as such it has been used throughout all time. Its first masters appear to have looked upon it as a kind of altar for their religious offerings; later, the Roman legionaries built a watch-tower, possibly a fortress, on its summit, and the saying has it that in 816 Pepin, the son of Charlemagne, claimed it as his own. It would take us too far to follow its succeeding history, and I can only advise those whose interest may have been aroused to read Scheffel's romance of *Ekkehard*, and there learn the story of the ruined monastery, of its foundress the beautiful Herzogin Hadwiga, of

48

the monk whose mad love for her made him forget his vows, of his punishment and of his rescue at her hands. The story, based on the chronicles of the monk, Ekkehard IV., is one of the poet's greatest works, and it surrounds Hohentwiel with the light of a half-real, half-legendary romance. Later on, in the Thirty Years' War, the castle of the Hohentwiel won high renown for itself under the command of Konrad Wiederhold, who defended it successfully for fifteen years against the Imperial troops, and at the concluding peace was able to hand it over unconquered to his master the Duke of Wurtemberg. This glory was overshadowed by its surrender to Napoleon in 1800, who had it razed to the ground. From that date its history as a fortress ends, but its interest remains, and the view from the summit of the rock should compensate every weary climber for his pains. The whole land of the Hegau lies beneath him, broken every here and there in its smooth, green undulations by other abrupt, almost unnatural-looking elevations. There are seven of these strange rocky formations—the Howenegg, Neuenhowen, Hohenhowen, Hohenstoffeln, Mandelberg, Hohenkrähen, and Hohentwiel. The neighbours of the last-named lie northwards almost in a direct line, as though Nature had intended to erect a barrier of

D 49

fortresses, and as such they have all been used, as the ruins on their summits testify. Each is well worth a visit if the traveller has time to spare, for each has its history, its ghosts, and its goblins; but the Hegau and its volcanic mountains mark only the entrance to the Black Forest, and we, knowing that the Hohentwiel was the limit of our experiences in this region, made the most of its interest and of the wide-spreading view of the Alps and the Black Forest lying before us in the light and shadow of a fading sunset. Afterwards, the stumble down through the half darkness successfully reduced us to a state of weariness which subdued all longings for the pleasures of an hotel drawing-room, and made the really comfortable beds of our simple little Gasthaus wholly acceptable.

The next morning was to see our arrival at Boll per automobile. To tell the truth, the prospect, as held out to us by our mentor of the gold-braided cap, rather alarmed us. We were simple ramblers with simple tastes, and visions of Mercédès cars with haughty chauffeurs and a mighty bill of costs hovered before our mental vision. We ventured to make inquiries, and on hearing that the price of a four-hours' ride amounted to the humble amount of thirty marks—all included—our fears rather increased than diminished. We felt that we must have misunderstood, or that there was deceit in the business, and waited in some suspense. And then presently, as we stood waiting for our Mercédès on the doorstep of the hotel, a great commotion broke the peaceful morning's silence —a shrill bugle note, then the call of a trumpet, such as might announce the arrival of a rescuing Lohengrin, then a fearful rattle and chain-clanking, and our Mercédès snorted round the corner. We understood then, and it must be confessed that our fears changed their character. Should we ever reach our destination—alive? But it was too late to consider. The Mercédès stood there waiting for us, for all the world like an animated pill-box, red in the face, and shaking in every bolt with impatience, the owner and chauffeur—a most elegant man and quite the smartest chauffeur I have ever seen in the way of 'get up'—was haughtily superintending the difficult task of stowing away our small box on the minute seat beside him, and a crowd of solemn urchins had assembled to watch the departure of *The Motor*.

There was no help for it, our fate was sealed and we could not but trust ourselves to Providence. Our progress through Singen was triumphant. There being no hills to encounter, our little car snorted along at a high rate of speed—possibly as much as fourteen miles an hour—and the loud tooting of our horn, which, having about ten notes in its register, achieved quite Wagnerian motifs, brought out half the town to admire and wonder. Afterwards, when we had left Singen behind us, and the admiring audience had disappeared, our pace decreased considerably. The horn ceased from troubling, and the car pulled all its eight horse-power together for its task.

The country before us rose steadily, so that we were on our second gear the whole time, except when we passed through the peaceful villages which here and there broke the monotony of our road. Only the absolute sang-froid and confidence of our chauffeur kept us from despair, and it must be admitted he knew how to make use of every atom of his possession. He knew exactly how to coax her up the steepest encline, and when at last we reached the highest point of our ascent he turned and smiled upon us with undisguised triumph.

"Goes well, nicht wahr?" he said. "Ach! but next year I shall have one with twenty horse-power, and then you will see!"

We expressed such admiration that his previous reserve melted, and he condescended to point out to us the beauty of our surroundings We ourselves had mounted the northern end of the Hohen Randen. Behind us lay the Hegau with

its rounded, sparsely wooded hills; to the left
the Hohen Randen; to the right, in the far
distance, a dark outline of forest, and beneath us
the valley of the Wutach.   From where our
car stood panting and shaking like a tired
horse, the road downwards looked like a winding ribbon, and the valley a narrow, rocky cleft,
overshadowed by a rough growth of trees.
There was, indeed, something perilous in our
descent, rapid and curving as it was, but the
brakes held good, and we felt, as we swept into
the shade and under the great viaducts of the
Black Forest railway, that we were really entering into our promised land.   From thence our
road lay on the level through the wild, romantic
valley whose acquaintance we determined to
renew; past the villages of Blumegg and
Weizen, our engine all this time working with
unwonted ease and energy.   But the hour of
its trial was yet to come; once again came a
big rise of open ground, the wooded ravines
lay behind us, and slowly but steadily we
neared the village of Bonndorf.   Perhaps, thanks
to its exposed position, the village is of comparatively late origin; once the seat of a long
extinct nobility, it passed into the possession of
St. Blasien and has little history of interest
to relate.   A bell in Bonndorf's coat-of-arms
recalls a legend of a certain Fräulein von Tanegg,

53

who, losing her way one wild winter's night, was only saved by the ringing of a prayer bell from the Pauliner Monastery. In gratitude she presented the chapel with a silver bell, but as monastery, town, and bell were all destroyed by the fires to which Bonndorf seems to have been unfortunately subject, no proof of the legend is left. As the village stands to-day, it offers but little interest to the traveller, and we passed on our way to our final destination.

With Bonndorf we seemed to leave the last trace of the Hegau's unwooded land behind us and to enter into a new world. A narrow road, cut through the very heart of the Forest, led downwards with a threatening steepness which made even our chauffeur shake his head doubtfully. He was the more doubtful since the district was new to him, and he could scarcely believe that there was a human habitation to be found in all this loneliness. In the distance we could hear the muffled roar of a swollen river, and then with a suddenness to which one grows gradually accustomed in the Black Forest, the road ended, and a pleasant-looking white-washed house, with 'Bad-Boll' written in large letters over its inviting face, told us that our day's journey was at an end.

There is nothing more agreeable than arriving at a genuine old Black Forest hotel. It is true that there are no great comforts or luxuries, but the host and his wife come out to greet you with a kindly warmth, and display a personal, yet always respectful interest in your welfare, which does the modern traveller good, accustomed as he is to the impersonal and casual ways of fashionable hotel proprietors. At any rate we were glad enough to descend from our close quarters and bid our sturdy little car and its amiable owner farewell. Though a trifle bone-shaken we could honestly say that we owed them a few pleasant hours and a wider view of the country than would have been possible from the railway carriage—both at a price which put us a little to shame. And thus my advice to any traveller who may chance to follow our route is this : when at Singen ask for Singen's motor car ! There can be no mistake —there is but one !

CHAPTER V

BOLL AND THE VALLEY OF THE WUTACH

LULLED by the soft, unceasing chatter of the river that flowed close beneath our window, and perhaps a trifle intoxicated by the strong air which had been blown to us from over the Hohen Randen during our breakneck motor drive, we spent our first night in Bad-Boll in dreamless sleep. I must even confess that Frau Sonne had already sent more than one full ray into the valley before we made our descent into the large, airy dining-room of the simple Gasthaus—to find, to our shame, that we formed the tail of late risers. Yet possibly we had an excuse, for there is indeed something in the atmosphere of Bad-Boll which acts like an opiate on the exhausted nerves of town children. Even compared to the quiet of dreamy little Singen the peace of the place is at first almost numbing. The village lies twenty minutes away; there is no high-road and not a house or cottage to lighten the sense

56

of absolute loneliness ; on either hand the walls
of the ravine—for it is more ravine than valley
—rise up to six hundred feet of part rock, part
fir-covered grandeur, completely shutting out
the world, and only the unchanging voice of the
mysterious Wutach breaks the silence. And
after a time even that sound seems to pass
away : it becomes part of the hearer's self, so
that he ceases to notice it, and the silence
becomes absolute. We felt, indeed, as we gazed
about us that this was the end of the world, but
not a sad or gloomy end. The pale Black Forest
sunshine (the sunshine in the Black Forest is
different from the sunshine anywhere else in the
world), falling slantways on to the western wall
and creeping slowly down the river, awoke such
warm and lively colours that we felt rather that
this end of the world belonged to an unexplored
fairyland, and that we, having discovered it,
had the right to claim it as our own. I fancy
that is the feeling of most of Boll's visitors.
The place is so little known, so little advertised,
that its clientèle is composed chiefly of ramblers
who in past years came upon it by chance, and,
charmed by its beauty and peace, have come
again, bringing their friends, and growing gradually to take a proprietary interest in its welfare.
We realised this peculiarity on our first morning,
for, as we stood on the steps of the hotel, un-

decided as to which direction our first ramble should take, we were accosted in English by a middle-aged gentleman who had been watching us for some time with a half-friendly, half-suspicious interest. After having accused us of being strangers to the place, he asserted his superiority and authority by informing us that he had been a regular guest at Boll for the last twenty years, that it was the most beautiful spot in the Black Forest, and that he knew every corner of it. We ventured thereupon to inquire how it came about that, in spite of its retired position and few claims to fashionableness, Boll seemed so favoured by English folk—himself included. He smiled and pointed to the river.

"That is the reason," he said. "Once upon a time Boll belonged to an English fishing club, which still takes an interest in the place, though the fishing is not what it was." He shook his head regretfully. "Still, the trout is excellent—you will find out that for yourselves. And, anyhow, people who come here always come again —if they are the right sort, of course."

I imagined that by the 'right sort' he meant genuine ramblers, people who prefer the interest and beauty of their surroundings to luxurious table d'hôtes and all the details of a fashionable hotel life. At any rate, when we told him that we were but waiting for an inspiration before

58

setting out on a tour of exploration, his manner softened and he directed us to visit the Lothenbachklamm, about an hour's walk from Boll.

"It is the most beautiful waterfall in the Black Forest," he reiterated proudly.

The prospect of a two-hours' ramble before dinner pleased our fancy. We bade our enthusiastic Englishman farewell, and leaving him engaged with his fishing tackle, we proceeded along the narrow road down which our motorcar had brought us the previous day. For ten minutes our way led upwards through a green glade of pine and fir, then, guided by the kindly signposts which never fail the traveller even in the most lonely regions of the Black Forest, we turned to the left and once more our view opened out on to the Wutach, now a hundred feet or so beneath us. From thence our road curved gracefully downwards to the river bank, and if the reader wonders at this up-and-down route, he need only consider the nature of the valley to understand why it is that only here and there has it been possible for the indefatigable Schwarzwald Verein to win a pathway at the side of the unruly Wutach. For the valley is more or less the work of the river, a cleft cut through the soft chalk rock by the waters, and consequently in places so narrow, so wild and rugged, that there is scarcely more than

a foothold left for the traveller, who in earlier
days had either to wade his way as best he could,
or keep to the road above the valley, contenting
himself with an occasional glimpse into the abyss
beneath. Hence it is not surprising that in
spite of its unusual length—it is the longest
river in the Black Forest, measuring 112 kilometres—and its many unusual characteristics,
it remains one of the least known and one of
the least visited. Taking its source on the
heights of the Feldberg, and bearing the names
of Rothwasser and Seebach, it flows into the
Titisee, and from thence north-east, this time
re-christened, as is the bewildering habit of
Black Forest rivers, with the name 'Gutach.'
As it at last chooses its final course south-east,
Gutach becomes 'Wutach,' and under that
name the river and its valley take on a character
of romantic ruggedness. In spite of its extreme
inaccessibility, it has known habitation, as the
ruins on its rocky walls testify. Two castles,
those of Stallegg and Neublumberg, are to be met
on the road from Boll to the village of Gösch-
weiler, but time and history have dealt hardly
with both, for little is left to see and still less to
relate. I confess that Stallegg seemed likely to
remain *terra incognita* for us, it lying beyond a
comfortable day's ramble, and had it not been
for our English mentor—but sufficient for the

day is—the pleasure thereof; and on this, our first day in Boll, our adventurous spirit took us no farther than the Lothenbachklamm. Our pleasant winding road having brought us once more to the river's edge, we paused a moment to consider the Schatten Muhle (Shadow Mill), so called because it is left sunless throughout the long winter, and then turned to the left up a mossy pathway. A merry, impatient little brook, hurrying on its way to join the Wutach, acted unconsciously as our guide, and a few minutes later the peaceful glade through which we were making our way closed in; our path mounted steadily up along a rocky wall in whose crevices a wonderful luxuriant growth of rare ferns and forest flowers had managed to find root. Below us our harmless brook revealed itself as a stormy torrent cascading from fall to fall, churning itself in a white foam of rage against the polished rock, and swirling over the trunks of fallen pine trees which barred its path. From one side of this little ravine to the other it could not have measured more than a few yards, and the spray brushing our faces hung on the ferns, and danced like tiny diamonds through the sunshine which here and there had managed to creep its way amidst the over-shadowing pines. We stood a moment in rapt delight, and I ventured to remark that the scenery reminded me of the Wolf's Schlucht in Weber's *Freischütz*, that, in fact, it reminded me strongly of theatre decorations ; whereupon, as I might have expected, my German friend sniffed contemptuously.

"English people are so artificial in their taste that they can see nothing without the medium of art," she declared. "If you must make comparisons why don't you say that theatre decorations remind you of *this*?" But being incurably English I continued in my way of thinking, and, indeed, the Lothenbachklamm is, in its minuteness, so perfect, so worked out in every detail, that it is scarcely possible to believe that careless Nature and not an artist hand seeking for 'effect' has carved the rocks and planted the ferns, and arranged the dark fir trees for a background with such seeming cunning. Even animal life has not been forgotten in the scheme of things. A gorgeous butterfly, coming apparently from nowhere, has chosen out the flaring red fruit of a wild strawberry on which to rest its wings ; a lizard of many changing hues flashes across the path and hesitates, like a stone image, on a jutting rock above the torrent, and one wonders, being English, is it done on purpose, is there not some wily stage-manager behind the scenes pulling the wires for our delectation ? But, as may be imagined, I kept this sacrilegious thought to myself and followed my critic, who by this time had reached the top of the 'klamm' and was considering the possibilities of a path which, tending due east, promised to return to Boll. It fulfilled its promise, but, alas! the season was still young, the path untrodden, the grasses long, and rain, as usual, had been of recent date. Hence it was in a sodden and somewhat uncomfortable condition that we presently found ourselves back on the high-road. And to this incident hangs a moral — take with you, O rambler, as many pairs of stout waterproof boots as your purse can buy and your luggage allows! Well kept as the Black Forest paths usually are, there are still places where one stands in need of stout footwear, especially in the less travelled regions which we are now exploring; and in addition to this, as our offering to the capricious weather god I venture to advise a mantle of the well-known 'Loden' material. The latter is light, warm, and waterproof, and adds immensely to one's general comfort, as we discovered after three or four drenchings and as many unpleasant experiences with the ordinary mackintosh. At any rate, the condition of our shoe department warned us that ordinary walking material was of little good for our requirements, and that same day, having sought the advice of our kindly hostess, we made our way in the direction of Bonndorf, the one possible shopping-place of the district. The time was not wasted, however, for the path which leads up from the left of the ordinary road is pleasantly shaded with fir and silver beech, and gives the wanderer, every here and there, a glimpse into narrow ravines, overgrown with moss and wild shrub which seem to cling to the rocks by sheer force of will, and to have their roots no one knows where. To the right of the path, half hidden by the trees, we discovered the ruins of Burg Boll. Only a few walls remain of what was once the home of defence of the knights of Bell. The race appears to have died out in the fourteenth century and the property to have fallen into the hands of their neighbours of Schloss Tanegg, but how the Burg came to be destroyed no one knows. Probably a collapse of the rocks on which the place is built offers the best explanation.

A few minutes' walk brought us to the village of Boll, a quiet little nest which, if one may judge from the inscriptions in the churchyard, has remained for generations in the hands of three or four families. Straight through the village our road led us up over the brow of a hill, and once again it seemed to us that we had left the Black Forest behind us and were once

more in the region of the Hegau. Before us
an endless stretch of undulating ground rolled
southwards, broken here and there by a patch
of wooded land, and only when we turned to
look back on the road we had come could we
believe in the proximity of the Forest. From
beneath us in the valley it stretched out to
the gray horizon, a seemingly black, unbroken
shadow, and yet we knew well enough the
countless valleys, rivers, mountains, and chasms
which it hid in its apparent monotony, and felt
for the first time the awe which the Black
Forest can inspire. It seemed, indeed, to us in
that moment very *black*, the abode of strange
spirits and wild beasts, a place of dark wonders
and mystery; and possibly we should have
stood there dreaming ourselves into a thoroughly
'creepy' state had not the boots recalled us to
our duty. Ten minutes' walk over the brow of
the hill brought us to Bonndorf itself. After a
few inquiries we discovered the shop of which
we were in search, and out of the midst of
sugar-candy, coloured handkerchiefs, sausages,
and cheese, succeeded in obtaining our requirements. I feel it only just to mention in consideration of their service, that they were—and
are—the most wonderful boots I have ever
bought. They cost nine marks, are indestruct-
ible, comfortable, watertight — and hideous.

But the latter feature is easy to forgive in the Black Forest, where only utility counts and fashionable clothes are almost a breach of good taste.

Having partaken of a cup of coffee at the Gasthaus zur Post, we left Bonndorf and its rustic Whiteley's behind us, and started on our way home. The threatening clouds of the afternoon had now dispersed, and tempted by the evening sunshine we ventured along a path which, after the wanderer has passed the Boll ruins, turns abruptly to the left, and leading over a half-dried-up waterfall brings him to the Castle of Tanegg. Here also history maintains a silence which we hope speaks well for the castle's possessors, who seem to have changed many times, until at last the religious orders in St. Blasien, always on the alert for such 'bon bouches,' pounced on the lordless property and made it their own. From the ruin downward the path leads back to the valley of the Wutach, which here has broadened out somewhat and taken on a momentary appearance of almost pastoral peace. But the appearance is deceptive, as we learnt on the following day. For a quarter of an hour after we had left Bad-Boll, the path along the right bank of the river offered no difficulties, but beyond the point which we had reached on our return from Burg

Tanegg the valley closes in abruptly; on the right hand towers a jagged precipice, against whose base the Wutach churns in impatient fury, making the continuation of the path an apparent impossibility. Until a short time ago this part of the Wutach was closed to the ordinary rambler, and only an occasional angler, taking the chance offered by a low state of the river, ventured to wade his way round the bends and explore the solitudes beyond. Then came the indefatigable Schwarzwald Verein and built the costly and arduous Neumann's Weg, a narrow path cut out of the face of the precipice and guarded at the edge by a slender wooden rail. The place, though absolutely safe in daylight, has already claimed its victims. The fall of the first, a young peasant, is attributed to a too jubilant condition, but a cloud of mystery veils the second accident, and the death of a young Englishman, who was found lying on a rock at the foot of the precipice, has been vaguely connected with robbery and murder and other horrors. The spot is certainly lonely and wild enough to foster fancies of that kind, though I confess that we experienced no adventure of particularly thrilling qualities. At first, rising by roughly hewn stone steps, the path reaches almost the summit of the precipice, then, winding round the face of the rock, descends into a shadowy glade, and leads across an iron bridge to the left bank of the river. Before we reached our destination, the Wutach Mill, we crossed the river three times, the third time pausing a moment to watch the Wutach, which at this point, in fact, disappears into a cavity at the base of the rock. Had we not known of this phenomena we should probably have passed it by unnoticed, for the cavity lies so low that the swiftly running waters touch the roof, and only a sharp eye can discern its existence. Farther on we passed the turning which leads away from the Wutach to the village of Bachheim, but the love of adventure was on us and the increasing loneliness of the valley tempted us on. . Once again a bridge brought us on to the right bank, where the path had been cut at the base of the cliff, so that, with the towering rock on one hand and the river on the other, a single-file progress became necessary. A few paces farther on the Wutach reappears from its long, underground journey and rushes out from beneath the cliff with a triumphant roar. To the left a wooden bridge leads into the Gauchachschlucht (Gauchach's Gorge), and our good angel suggesting to us that this new road might offer new attractions, we were about to cross the river and track its territory, the Gauchach, as far as the Loch Mühle, when an evil genius, in

the form of a well-meaning friend, who was
wading about in midstream in the hope of
deceiving hungry trout, began a eulogy on the
merits of the Wutach Mühle, a quarter of an
hour farther on the road. We protested that
we were tired and had not the slightest desire
to go back the same somewhat arduous way as
we had come, but our enthusiastic friend, as is
the fashion with such folk, remained obdurate.

" You will be able to get dinner and a carriage
at the Mill," he said. " The drive home over
Bonndorf is delightful."

We were weak, and from this point our
experiences are related simply with the purpose
of explaining 'how not to do it.' Had we
obeyed our first impulse we should have had
a pleasant walk through a charming valley—
passing on the way the Burg Mühle, made
celebrated by Scheffel's " Juniperus "—to the
Loch Mühle, and from thence, wandering off
from the Gauchach through wooded land and
pasture, reached Döggingen. At Döggingen the
railway takes the rambler to Reiselfingen, an
hour's walk from Bad-Boll over the Schatten
Mühle. All this we discovered later on and
only after bitter experience. For in the matter
of rambles, as in everything else, taste differs,
and it must be admitted that the continuation
of the Wutach Valley and the Wutach Mill

offered no particular attraction. The valley widens out and loses its romance and rugged grandeur. The Mill is a mill like hundreds of others, and the promised carriage proved a delusion ; or, rather, the carriage existed substantially enough, but the horses were missing, which, as mine host shrewdly observed, was a decided objection to our plan of being driven home.

"However, you will find carriages at Ewattingen," he said hopefully ; "a quarter of an hour up that hill and there you are ! "

Now my German friend is of an optimistic temperament, and in spite of repeated deceptions she still believes trustingly in her fellow-creatures and their 'quarters of an hour.'

Wearied in body, and haunted by a vague distrust, I followed her up the steep hill through the midday sun, counting the minutes, which reached thirty, before a church spire told us that Ewattingen was really in sight.

"Now, you see," said my German friend, " our troubles are at an end."

She was mistaken. The hostess of the little Gasthaus where we sought information shook her head with maddening cheerfulness.

"Ach ! ja," she said, " there are carriages enough, but there isn't a horse in the village. They are all in the fields, you know. Where have you come from ? "

FIELD WORKERS.

We told her, and she looked at us with kindly, half-pitying wonder. It appeared that the good old soul had never been outside her native village, and it is certain that she thought us a little mad. Possibly, therefore, it was compassion for our obviously weak mental state which made her send inquiries through the whole village, and presently she returned to us with her withered, furrowed old face bright with enthusiasm.

"An ox-wagon is going to the fields towards Münchingen," she said. "If you would like to use that, it will take you on your way."

"How far is Bonndorf from Münchingen?" I inquired.

She smiled a vague, sweet smile.

"Ach! Fräulein, a little half-hour, no more."

We followed her out into the street, where a crowd of bare-footed little urchins awaited our departure with profound interest. The ox-wagon—a Leiterwagen, as it is called—was also there, harnessed, not to oxen but to cows, who appeared to join dreamily in the general amusement. Now a Black Forest Leiterwagen is a vehicle of peculiar build. Take two long ladders with the rungs well apart, fasten them slantways on either side of a narrow plank, so that they form a kind of barricade, attach four wheels to this erection, and your carriage is complete. These Leiterwagen are used to transport hay from the fields, and are not intended for the use of weary travellers, as we soon discovered. With kindly consideration our hostess spread newspapers over the bottom of the cart, and instructed us how we were to sit with our feet dangling through the rungs of a ladder. I cannot blame the yokel who drove us for the half-smothered guffaw which I am certain I heard eminate from his direction, for we must have made a striking picture as we jolted out of the village at the rate of two miles an hour. My German friend, though she was as hungry and weary as myself, gloried in the situation, but my good humour wholly deserted me. I felt injured, and my sense of injury increased with her good spirits, so that it was with a positively spiteful satisfaction that a quarter of an hour later I heard our charioteer inform her, in his strongest dialect, that our ways parted and that we must go on foot.

"And how far is Bonndorf?" my German friend inquired cheerfully, as she pressed a silver piece of gratitude into his horny palm. It was clear that she expected Bonndorf to be 'just round the corner.'

Our friend scratched his head thoughtfully.

"Maybe three hours," he said. "It's straight on—you can't miss the way. A little over three hours," he added, as he turned his attention to his team.

The rest is silence. We reached Bad-Boll three hours later, having been rescued on the hot, dusty high-road by a most shaky but most welcome vehicle, which in its distant youth might have been a gentleman's victoria and had sunk to the position of a village maid-of-all-work. Our good-natured Lohengrin took us as far as Bonndorf, and from thence we resumed our trudge to Boll, thankful, but chastened in spirit, and hungry past all expression. Only after a good dinner were we able to 'fight our battles o'er again,' and it was fortunate for our angling friend that he appeared after the last course, otherwise our friendship might have ended there and then. Thus ended our rambles down-stream.

The Wutach continues on its changing way past the ruins of Schloss-Blumegg, once the residence of a powerful race, to Grimmelshofen. From Grimmelshofen the valley loses its interesting character, and the traveller can make use of the railway, which is of comparatively recent construction, and which, with its spiral tunnels, forms one of the most interesting engineering features of the Black Forest, without fear of losing any scenic beauties. For our part we turned our attention westwards, and after having impatiently waited through two days of bad weather, started one fine morning along the road towards the Schatten Mühle. The tour which we had planned for ourselves was calculated to require more than five hours' steady walking, so, warned by previous experiences, we took refreshment with us, thus making ourselves independent of doubtful inns.

We had already traversed the ground as far as the Schatten Mühle; at this point we crossed the bridge, and, after two and a quarter hours' walking, reached the ruins of what the natives call the Rauberschlossle (Robber's Castle), which is situated on the Nagelefelsen, and from whence a beautiful view can be obtained of the valley beneath. At this point it occurred to us that our eatables were getting cumbersome and that the situation merited half an hour's intermezzo, an idea which was immediately acted upon. Only a general distrust of guide-books aroused us from our pleasant dreams amongst the ruins, for though we were informed that the rest of our road required only two hours, 'we had our doots.' However, true to guide-book calculation, after two hours we reached the Schwendiholzdobel Bridge, which ought to be famous if only on account of its breakneck name, and had the pleasure of being introduced to the Wutach, under its new name of Gutach.

74

The river Haslach streams in from the left, but
our path lay onward by the banks of our re-
christened friend till half an hour later we
reached the railway bridge—the biggest stone
bridge in Germany—and crossing to the right
bank attained our destination, Kappel. Kappel
proved to be a small village, offering little
accommodation to the hungry and weary, so
that, in spite of a fine view over to the heights
of the Feldberg, we determined on a last effort.
Half an hour along the dusty high-road brought
us to Lenzkirch, and there, indeed, our courage
was rewarded. For this pleasant little summer
resort has an appearance of peaceful prosperity
which is most restful, and which, combined with
a good meal at the Gasthaus zum Adler, successfully restored us to a state of 'sweet content.'
Not that we despised the yellow 'post-chaise'
which was to carry us back to Bonndorf, for our
energy was of a subdued kind, and we parted
from Lenzkirch with a reluctance based, I fear,
on a certain inclination not to bestir ourselves.
Still, two and a half hours in a shaky Black
Forest post-chaise is calculated to satisfy the
most lazy, and Bonndorf once reached we were
perfectly satisfied to descend and stretch our
cramped limbs in the short walk back to Bad-
Boll. We had come to look upon the cleanly,
comfortable, if unpretentious little Gasthaus

very much in the light of a home, and it was with real regret that we remembered that the next day was to witness our departure for pastures new. In gratitude for one of the most pleasant weeks spent in the Black Forest, I feel it only right to recommend the rambler to seek this little-known spot—that is to say, if he is in need of peace, beautiful walks, and a fine, invigorating air. And if he is something of a sportsman, so much the better, for there is fishing in abundance ; and even the huntsman will find occupation enough in the surrounding forest. Many weeks could be spent in Bad-Boll without monotony — provided the visitor is armed with a sufficient library to while away the rainy days—but our plans forbade us making the experiment, and on the same evening of our walk to Lenzkirch we bade our various friends good-bye. Our angling friend looked at us pityingly,—he was there for two months,—our English acquaintance turned his back on us. I think he looked upon our departure as a personal insult.

CHAPTER VI

ST. BLASIEN AND THE ALB VALLEY

RARELY did we bless the sunshine more than on the following morning when, at eight o'clock, our host informed us that the carriage waited. For we had decided on the extravagance of a long drive to our next stopping-place, and the whole joy thereof lay in the hands of the weather-god. Fortunately he was in a holiday mood, and it was with the sense of pleasurable antici-pation that we took our places in the comfortable victoria and bade Bad-Boll farewell. The whole household had turned out to witness our depar-ture, and for once in a way we felt justified in flattering ourselves that it was not only thoughts of likely 'Trinkgelder' which aroused this in-terest, but that the host's handshake and 'God-speed' had the value of genuine kindly feeling. At any rate, useless as such gifts are on such occasions, we treasured the bouquet of wild flowers offered us at the last moment by a small member of the family until its faded condition

77

compelled us to consign it to the roadside—a dark deed of ingratitude which we fondly hoped escaped the eye of our driver.

In spite of our two sturdy horses our progress along the hilly roads promised to be a slow one, and on that account the more enjoyable, for though professed pedestrians we could not shut our hearts against the unalloyed pleasure of watching the lovely wooded country slip past us without any exertion or worry on our parts. Indeed, if I might once more commit the error of proffering advice, I would suggest that the traveller, when journeying from one place to another, should first inquire concerning the driving accommodation before consigning himself to the railway. I am supposing that the traveller is not a fanatic rambler—that is to say, a person determined to do it all on foot, with the barest toilette necessities strapped in a bundle to his back—but a person who likes to go his way in average comfort, in which case it is very often cheaper and certainly more agreeable to drive than to go by rail. Our journey to St. Blasien is a case in point. Had we chosen the latter course we should have had to drive to Bonndorf, undergo a long, zigzag railway journey, and at the end had an expensive drive from the nearest station to St. Blasien. As it was, we paid the comparatively small sum of twenty marks, and were transported with all our goods and chattels to our destination in the utmost comfort. The new insight which it gave us into the beauty of the country alone made the drive worth while.

After we left Bonndorf behind us the character of the scenery seemed imperceptibly to change. It was no longer the wild, almost jungle-like grandeur of the Wutach Valley, and yet it became more 'typical'; the Black Forest, as we already knew it from previous rambles, seemed to be closing us in on all sides. Even when our carriage reached the highest points of land we found no open country breaking the shadow of forest-land which stretched to the horizon, and already on the winding, sometimes grass-grown road we felt that first genuine touch of shadow and mystery which has made the Black Forest a place of legend and fairy-tale. Not that the shady avenues offered us as yet the final impenetrable, sunless darkness to which the Forest owes its name. Leafy birch and silver beech mingled with the more solemn olive of the pines, and the cool morning sunshine, falling aslant between the branches, lit up an undergrowth of moss and giant fern. We passed few villages on our way, and the usual broken train of ramblers and carriages failed wholly. We were, in fact, following an unusual route, one altogether ignored by guide-books, but not the less beautiful for that, and we allowed' the absolute peace and quiet to work like a charm upon our mood.

Not that we were altogether alone. With silent touch on the arm and a pointed finger we drew each other's attention to the squirrels scuttling noiselessly up the trunks of the trees, to the deer which here and there trotted out of the heart of the Forest to watch us with a curiously fearless interest. I have heard Black Forest detracters declare that there is no animal life to be found there, and that the Forest never hears the sound of a bird's note. During this drive to St. Blasien we gathered evidence enough to refute this statement, though I confess that the animal life is of a quiet kind—perhaps not obvious enough for the tourist. At first glance, as it were, nothing moves, everything about you is wrapped in a profound hush. Then first you begin to hear the music among the pine-tops, and gradually sounds seem to rise up around you out of the stillness—the call of the ring-doves, the far-off voice of the cuckoo, and suddenly the full song of the thrush. The thrush is the great singer of the Black Forest —possibly, with the blackbird, the only singer, for therein the tourist has truth on his side —the forest singers are few. Possibly the shadows are too deep for them, or, still more likely, the companionship of the birds of prey too threatening. For it is certain that the nightingale whose song once made Freiburg and the surrounding country famous has been entirely destroyed by the rapacity of the blackbird, and though the blackbird is scarcely a bird of prey, her tricks of thieving and ruthlessly destroying makes her almost as dangerous. Falcons, too, abound, especially about the walls of old ruins, and owls are the plentiful causes of the gloomy superstitions among the peasants, who look upon them as sure omens of a coming death. And there is the famous Auerhahn, the speciality of the Black Forest, of whom I shall speak later when we come to his region. And the stork! I suppose a whole volume could be written about the patron saint of South Germany— for that is about what he amounts to. You will find him and his family in almost every village in the valleys and occasionally in the mountains, and wherever he deigns to settle himself and his belongings he is looked upon with the greateat respect and treated like a prince who has come from far-off lands for a summer 'Kur' with his princess. Possibly this love and respect with which Herr Storch is regarded is owing to the fact that he is a reputed importer of babies—at any rate, his nest is always prepared for him upon his favourite roof, and the house upon whose chimney he has cast favourable eyes is as good as blessed with every blessing. On the whole, the animal world of the Black Forest is of a harmless enough kind. Wolves and bears breathed their last a hundred years ago, and the few wild boars which remain are hard to find, and unless irritated entirely inoffensive. The stag is also a rarity, but deer are often to be seen in the shady glades and seem comparatively at their ease in the presence of mankind. The squirrel, too, is a constant apparition, as also the hare, and in the region of rivers and brooks the otter makes himself unpopular by competing with the hotel-keepers in the matter of trout, thereby sending up the price of that delicacy by leaps and bounds. Not that I look on trout any longer as a delicacy, for the Black Forest traveller has the little fish served up to him every Thursday and Sunday (German hotel feast-days) with a wearying regularity which begets contempt, not to say distaste. However, there are worse things in the Black Forest than trout. There are snakes! I have often met them in the course of my rambles, and after the first shock can look upon them with a friendly interest.

For the most part they are harmless adders, sometimes attaining about four feet in length, and, like the salamanders and lizards which are to be found everywhere, change their colours when angered. And it is quite safe to anger them if you feel inclined to experiment, for their bite is non-poisonous. The one and only dangerous element is the common viper, which, paradoxically, is uncommon enough to make the danger of an almost negligible quality. I am now wandering in the realm of hearsay, for, personally, I have never met one of the gentry, but for safety's sake it is well, when on a sunny moor or in a ruin, to look round and make sure that an ugly flat head is not raised to strike. As a compensation for these possible unpleasantnesses there are the living flowers—the butterflies. There was a time when their beauty and profusion tempted me to purchase a net and a tin lethal chamber and go a-hunting, but in the end I gave it up. Possibly I am not scientific enough—as the reader may have discovered—to enjoy destruction for scientific reasons, possibly I thought it a pity to deprive the world of so much living loveliness, possibly I found it too exhausting. At any rate, the 2200 species, some of them unique, which have their home in the South Black Forest, have nothing more to fear from me, and I am afraid I have not the heart to encourage a prospective butterfly-catcher to follow my earlier barbaric footsteps. The unhappy creature, with a pin stuck through its delicate body, which adorns a glass case is nothing like so beautiful as the blue-winged wonder perched on the edge of a flower, with a background of green forest to throw up its rich colours into lovelier relief. My last word on the subject of life in the Black Forest belongs to the bee, who, like the stork, seems particularly connected with that country. But the rambler who knows the pine-honey will understand me, and the rambler who does not know it should make its acquaintance at the earliest possible date.

But the sight of the deer has led me very far from the road, and meanwhile the sun has risen high into the heavens and our two patient horses have drawn us up on to the high ground by Rothaus (famous for its brewery), and below us we see the winding road, which leads to our halting-place, Schluchsee. Another half-hour's drive brings us to the village (2858 feet), a charming little place; with reason, one of the most popular of Black Forest resorts. It lies within full view of the lake, and from the verandah of the Gasthaus, where we stopped for the refreshment of our horses, and incidentally for our dinner, we could look straight over the unruffled waters to the farther banks. As has been said, none of the Black Forest lakes attain any serious dimensions, but though the Schluchsee has nothing to offer as regards length and breadth, and lacks wholly the gloomy mystery and grandeur of a Feldsee, it has none the less its own charm and character. The banks run smoothly to the water's edge, there are no rocks or cliffs, only peaceful wooded stretches with here and there an open space of the gorse-grown land. In August, when the heather is in full bloom, the contrast in colour between the olive of the pine, the brilliant purple blossom, and the dark surface of the lake make a striking and beautiful effect. Yet in August the crowded hotels and the general atmosphere of 'holiday-making' spoil the peace and retirement of the place, so that we were well content to see the Schluchsee in its early summer dress. As it was, the village was already astir with guests, automobiles, bearing day visitors from St. Blasien, which stirred up the dust in the high-road; the lake was dotted with little boats, and from the number of amateur anglers who passed the open verandah on which we were partaking of the inevitable trout, we judged that the lake offered excellent fishing.

85

RAMBLES IN THE BLACK FOREST

On the whole a charming place in itself, with invigorating air and beautiful surroundings, but a trifle too near the big centres—such was our judgment, and being people not too fond of fellow-creatures in large quantities, we were willing enough to move on.

A pleasant drive brought us in the early afternoon to St. Blasien, and already when half an hour away from our destination our quiet-loving hearts began to sink with misgiving. We had heard a great deal of St. Blasien (2316 feet), of its lovely situation, its fine air and romantic history, and it was therefore rather foolish, not to say egoistical, of us to expect to have it all to ourselves. Certainly its popularity was obvious. Monstrous overladen tripper motor-cars, carriages, fashionable pedestrians, and stout Kurhaus guests met us on the road with increasing frequency, and by the time the dome of St. Blasien's church rose in sight, we were prepared for the worst.

The unfortunate part about rambles described from personal experiences is that the writer is bound to mention the disappointing experiences with the good, and it is always possible that his judgment of a place is influenced by an unlucky constellation of circumstances entirely peculiar to himself. At any rate, I hope I am not doing St. Blasien an injustice, or keeping

86

ST. BLASIEN.

a possible admirer from her regions by saying
that I, personally, was glad when we left the
valley behind us, and were able to look back
on the town—so beautiful from a distance—in
unregretting farewell. Certainly we were unfortunate in St. Blasien, and our misfortunes
began at once. In the first place, we could find
no rooms in the Kurhaus. Our friend of the
guide-book would tell us that that at least was
entirely our own fault, that one must always
book rooms in advance, etc. etc. ; but we had
a rooted objection to binding ourselves, and
though, as on this occasion, this happy-go-lucky
system has its disadvantages, it has also its more
weighty advantages, as the St. Blasien episode
eventually proved. We found rooms in another
hotel, but the overcrowded dining-room, the
newly evacuated bedrooms, the general atmosphere of bustle and confusion soured our
temper, and my German friend, who when
roused is wholly indifferent to ordinary con-
siderations, was for hoisting our boxes back
on to the carriage and fleeing anywhere, so long
as it was far from this 'fashionable health resort.'
However, reason prevailed, and after a gloomy
tea we proceeded to explore our new surroundings. Our first visit was to the church, and
my German friend, who had been storing her
mind with historical reminiscences, recovered her

temper somewhat in the satisfaction of airing her wisdom over my ignorance.

It appeared from her account that St. Blasien was one of the oldest and most important clerical centres of the Black Forest, and certainly her history typifies the whole history of the part played by the religious orders in these regions. At first, as we have seen in one of the first 'instructive chapters,' the part was beneficial enough.

Somewhere in the ninth century a party of monks, fleeing from the Huns, laid the first foundations of the future monastery, and having rescued the bones of St. Blasius from their pursuers, their place of refuge obtained already in those days a certain odour of sanctity. The danger past, however, these first pioneers apparently wearied of the loneliness and took their departure, leaving nothing behind them but the least important section of the holy skeleton. Thus for a few years St. Blasien languished. Then came the extraordinary and for our modern ideas scarcely conceivable tide of religious fanaticism, which swept the richest and greatest out of their worldly places into a life of solitude and renunciation. One of these world-weary folk, a certain Ritter von Seldenbeuren, discovered in St. Blasien a fitting place for his retirement, and having increased the

88

dimensions of the monastery, endowed it with considerable wealth. For some reason the place drew the attention of the Emperor Otto II., who bestowed great riches upon the monastery, which already had begun to exert a less beneficial authority over its surroundings. With the members of the highest nobility for its adherents, and an Imperial prince for its abbot, St. Blasien resembled more a royal court than a monastery, and luxury, greed, and cruelty took the place of the virtues for which it had been once famous. History even relates that the noble monks did not disdain violence and war and like methods for obtaining the possessions of their less powerful neighbours. It followed, as a natural consequence, that in the Peasants' War of 1525, St. Blasien was one of the first to pay the price of its transgressions, and the monastery was burnt to the ground. The same fate pursued it in the Thirty Years' War, and only under the abbot, Prince Martin, was it once more restored, this time in Italian style, and after the model of the Pantheon in Rome. A family vault for the members of the Habsburg house was erected in its midst, but in 1807 the abbot was finally deposed and the monastery converted into a manufactory. Even to-day, though the State has done much to restore it to its old splendour, the church, whose great dome stands out picturesquely against the dark green of the surrounding forest, is spoilt by the close proximity of the cotton-mill, and its effect is most striking from the heights of one of the enclosing mountains.

Having done our duty towards St. Blasien's ecclesiastical past, we spent the rest of the evening in the crowded streets and in grumbling. In truth St. Blasien is neither one thing nor another; it is too big for a village, too small for a town; too fashionable for the simple rambler, not fashionable enough or amusing enough for the ordinary society pleasure-seeker. Needless to say, there are pleasant shady walks in the neighbourhood, carefully laid out for the convenience of the guests, for the most part Germans of a rather objectionable class, but the very orderliness and comfort of these set walks takes away all charm. It is impossible to get away from one's fellow-creatures, and one seems to live in an unchanging atmosphere of hotel life. And the hotel life in such places as St. Blasien suffers from the complaint I have already mentioned. It has none of the simple, homely delights of Bad-Boll, and it falls far below the standard set by the people requiring the first and the best. Moreover, the prices, though not exorbitant—about 12 marks a day—are fairly high, considering what is offered, and I have

always found that in smaller places in the
Black Forest, where the average pension runs
from 7 marks to 9 marks, according to the
room and the season, the food is better and
the people more attentive. I might mention,
for the benefit of the rambler whose purse is
not the longest, that there are certain little
Gasthauser in the Black Forest where really
good food and spotless cleanliness can be
obtained for 4·50 a day. The menu comprises
a breakfast of coffee, rolls, butter, and honey,
a dinner of soup, fish, meat, and a simple
pudding, and a supper of meat and cheese.
Wine, is cheap and good—especially the open
wine, which can be had from 60 pfennig the
litre. Butter, milk, and honey are excellent
everywhere, and the smaller the place the more
the rambler can reckon on absolute cleanliness.
In such places as St. Blasien, where carpets and
the regulation plush furniture take the place
of the bare necessaries of a Bad-Boll, he has
reason to be more wary, though I have, personally,
nothing serious to complain of.

It is only fair at this juncture of my somewhat
unfavourable criticism concerning popular
St. Blasien, to state that the place is in itself
beautiful and worth visiting. Only, the visitor
should choose the very early season, when there
are fewer people and the atmosphere less

oppressive. Its closed in and sheltered position makes St. Blasien an admirable resort for the middle of June and even earlier, whereas in late July and August it has a decided tendency to stuffiness. For our part we determined on a short stay but a busy one, and the following day, being somewhat oppressed by the heat, we undertook the walk to Hochenschwand, which, standing at an elevation of 3000 feet, forms one of the highest villages in the Black Forest. Here, almost for the first time, we found a few cottages built after the typical Black Forest style; but we knew that more perfect specimens awaited us, and contented ourselves with the truly magnificent view. The Feldberg was now in sight; but, in spite of its superiority in feet and inches, it was only to be distinguished from its neighbours by the tower at the summit. As always in the Black Forest, we seemed to stand at the highest point, and to have the world at our feet, and the wind blowing in our faces had a keenness in it which recalled Alpine heights. In truth, Hochenschwand can rarely boast of a windless day, and the terrific storms for which it is noted makes the existence of the village and the hotel rather surprising. Towards the south we noticed the long, straight line of the Alb Valley, and since it is the only perceptible interruption in what seems an uninterrupted stretch of forest, we decided that it must be worth inspection. For we knew that there were valleys and jagged gorges enough in that seeming monotony, and consequently a valley which stood out from amongst the rest must possess both qualities of size and grandeur. Accordingly, the next day saw us setting out on our rambles, at the same time bidding St. Blasien farewell.

Our luggage had been sent on by the post-wagon to Albbruck, but we, determined to justify our claim to the title of ramblers, and tempted by the promised beauties of the valley, followed on foot. On the whole, I feel inclined to advise the more restful carriage. The distance measures a good fifteen miles, and if, as we were, the rambler has bound himself to catch a certain train at Albbruck, he may find himself too hurried and too tired to enjoy the full magnificence of the scenery. Certainly time should be allowed for a rest at the interesting village of Tiefenstein, which lies about two-thirds of the way on the road to Albbruck, and whose inn offers a good meal and lovely surroundings. From Tiefenstein onwards the valley assumes its most unusual and imposing aspect. Up to that point, though charming in its way, it differed in nothing particular from other Black Forest valleys. We passed the villages of

Kutterau and Immenreich, and then, about half-way, at a point where the valley begins to narrow and lose its pastoral aspect, the historic Nieder Mühle. This now peaceful-looking mill was the birthplace of Kanz Uehlin, one of the chief peasant leaders in the rising of 1525, whose capture and execution at the hands of the Austrian troops was the wind which blew the smouldering fire of hatred to a blaze. The final destruction of the monastery was the revenge of the enraged peasants on their oppressors.

Thus we reached Tiefenstein, tired and hungry, but sustained by the knowledge that the most beautiful part of our day lay before us. A good dinner at the Gasthaus, pleasantly situated by the bridge, refreshed us sufficiently to continue on our road, which now rose from the bed of the foaming Alb to a considerable height, and from thence curved round the summit of a narrow, rocky gorge. The view down into the cleft was wild and romantic enough to suit the most spoilt, and every here and there we had to pause to listen to the rushing waters below us as they roared and churned in white fury against the rocky walls of their prison. And during the brief stretches which hid the Alb from our view, I was regaled on legends and histories of Tiefenstein and its neighbourhood, so that when I peered down again into the sunless depths, it

94

seemed to me that I could see elves and goblins and the shadow of an emperor hovering in the white clouds of spray which rose up towards us. For these regions, which now seem so remote from all history, have often seen the great Rudolf of Habsburg and heard the clash of arms as he fought the bitter duel with the proud and noble race of the Tiefensteins. Their castle, whose ruins are still to be seen on a rock rising abruptly out of the meadows, saw the first scenes of that struggle whose history forms one of the most absorbing stories which the Spirit of the Black Forest has to tell us. Driven from their possessions by the then Count of Habsburg, the Tiefensteins barricaded themselves behind the walls of a tower in the neighbourhood of Kutterau and carried on a desperate robber warfare against their enemies of Habsburg and St. Blasien. It is said that one of the race founded a monastery where the river Ibach joins the Alb, but even his cloisters could not protect him from the covetous hatred of his family's deadly enemy. Rudolf drove the monks from their refuge and took their holy relic, the head of St. Cyrillus, to Hauenstein. Legend relates that in the following morning after this sacrilegious robbery the head was once more found on the altar of the monastery, and that Rudolf on hearing of this miracle was much frightened.

95

The same events were repeated, and this time the watchman who was posted to prevent any further trouble went mad. It is probable that Rudolf let the head have its own way. Nevertheless his war against the Tiefensteins continued until the day when the last of the proud, unfortunate race fell at the hands of one of his knights, leaving him complete master of their possessions. It was in these regions, too, that he seems to have felt the first stirrings of his ambition, for on the highlands above the Alb there is a mighty fir tree, greater than all her sisters, which legend has called the emperor's, since it was under her branches that Rudolf dreamed dreams of his great future. But his was not the only personality who interested the neighbourhood in those days.

There was an Alb king, half-fairy, half-goblin, who frequented the waters of a little lake near Tiefenstein and sang alluring songs—so alluring that if a pretty girl ventured to listen to them her senses left her and she sank for ever into the waters. For aught I know, this Alb king, unlike his better known rival of Habsburg, may be alive to-day, so that ramblers of the fair sex with pretensions to beauty should beware!

Thus beguiled with history and legend, carefully sandwiched by rests, during which I was made to admire the imposing loveliness of the

96

torrent beneath (how wonderful and worthy of long scrutiny a landscape becomes when one is tired!) we reached the hotel of Hohenfels.

The view of the foaming Alb from the hotel garden is perhaps the finest of all, and it is one of the great charms and peculiarities of this valley that from this point to the station, Albbruck, the road remains almost always directly on the edge of the precipice, so that the wanderer remains for the greater part of the time in full view of the torrent beneath. Certainly the beauty of this last half-hour's walk must have been of a bewitching character, for in spite of the fact that my walking powers are limited I reached Albbruck in a very fair temper, and was even able to appreciate the doubtful humour of the situation when the train for which we had been racing steamed out of the station at the same moment at which we entered it. Nor did I reproach my German friend for lingering in exclamatory admiration on the road—as I might have done. I was gracious. I suggested a cup of tea at the nearest Gasthaus, and the suggestion finding favour, we ended a successful ramble in peace and good-fellowship.

CHAPTER VII

THE WEHRA VALLEY: TODTMOOS
AND SURROUNDINGS

OUR train—or rather the train which took the
place of 'ours'—bore us on the same evening
to Wehr over Sackingen and Bennet. The
former town has little to offer in the way of
interest except the castle of Schönau with the
frescoes depicting scenes out of the *Trumpeter
of Säckingen*, Scheffel's most popular, if not
greatest poem. With Bennet the Wehra Valley
begins; but it was already late evening, and
knowing that at this point the scenery is of a
negligible quality we continued on our way as
far as Wehr, a little manufacturing village, or
town, as it perhaps calls itself, with a very
pleasant and hospitable Gasthaus situated
opposite the station. Our next long stopping-
place being Todtmoos (2496 feet), a village in
the heart of the mountains, we determined to
see everything which the neighbourhood had to
offer before leaving it for higher regions; and

98

HASEL.

the next morning, accordingly, we set off on foot for Hasel and the famous Erdmanshóhle (Earthman's Cave), the most celebrated of the Black Forest subterranean drop-stone caves. Apart from this phenomenon, Hasel is in itself a charming little village and well worth the three-quarters of an hour's walk which brings the traveller to its limits. It is typical of most lowland villages in the Black Forest. There are no straw-covered roofs and oaken beams, burnt black with sun and wind, as we were to find them later on in our travels, but there is a peaceful gaiety in the long, winding street with its white-washed cottages—and the gay-coloured shutters, crude enough in themselves, lend a touch of brilliancy to the scene. Nor are the people as yet 'typical' as Black Foresters, but they are a simple, friendly race, by their courteous dignity marked apart from the inhabitants of the busier towns. They are just 'country folk,' and the 'country folk' of South Germany — I hope my long-standing acquaintance with them does not prejudice me unduly—are surely the most charming in the world.

At the first inn which meets the traveller on the road, we inquired after a guide for the Erdmanshohle, and whilst the serving-girl rushed off to find the village schoolmaster, who, as usual, undertakes all such jobs, we refreshed ourselves with homely bread and cheese and a glass of country wine; thus strengthened, we then followed our guide over the pastures behind the village to the brow of a low hill, where an entrance cut into the rock led down into the subterranean passages. But first we had to be garbed in a fantastic hooded mantle, for, as in a certain poem, there is 'water, water everywhere,' and even if you are clever enough to avoid falling into the numerous pools you are certain not to escape the heavy drops which fall from the low roof. Thus attired, and looking ourselves not unlike earthmen, we proceeded down the steep flight of steps and left daylight and the summer warmth behind us. The cold is at first penetrating and damp, but 'on s'habitue à tout,' and after a few moments we ceased to notice the change of atmosphere. Certainly the Erdmanshohle is worth visiting, and even with the memories of Swiss wonders of the same type in our minds we were fain to confess that this was the most interesting we had seen. The long, water-carved galleries, the lakes, the chapels supported by gigantic pillars, the princes' vault with its carved coffins and tombs, the hundred and one quaint shapes and figures which seem to watch you as you pass, are in their way unique, and it is impossible to

suppress a sensation of awe when you realise
that you stand before the work of countless ages.
The passages are well lighted by electricity, and
our guide showed an almost proprietary pleasure
in pointing out to us the various marvels and
explaining to us the gradual formation of the
stone pillars. Most impressive of all was the
dull thunder of the river, at one point visible,
which flows underground, making, it is believed,
innumerable curves and twists before bursting
out half an hour later into the light of day. As
our guide informed us, the whole country round
is undermined with these secret waterways.
There is, for instance, on the 'Dinkelsberg,' a
small lake—the Eichener See—whose grey-blue
waters at times wholly disappear, at other times
return with a violence and suddenness which is
even threatening for the neighbouring village.
No fish can exist in its waters, and no flowers
or plants grow on its banks : only frogs and
toads inhabit its mysteries, which are dimly
supposed to be connected with those of the
Erdmanshohle. The latter cave measures 360
metres in length, so far as it is explorable to-day,
but there are probably miles more of territory
as yet unknown and probably for ever closed
against human curiosity, for the expenses of
the pioneer work are heavy, and the visitors so
few that it is doubtful if the necessary funds

will ever be forthcoming. After half an hour's wandering, we returned once more to the surface; the air, which had seemed to us only pleasantly warm before our descent, now seemed suffocatingly hot, and it was in rather a languid frame of mind that we set out on our way back to Wehr. Fortunately the road runs downhill most of the time, and my German friend's camera provided sufficient excuse for the sundry necessary rests, so that I at least was able to make proper use of the grassy banks on the wayside. (In case it be remarked that our 'staying powers' were not of a remarkable order, I should like to draw attention to the fact that we *had* performed marvels on the previous day, and that anyhow this book is *not* entitled *Pedestrian Records*! We rambled, and rambling in the genuine sense of the word never includes over-exerting oneself.) Having given this explanation, I trust the reader will be neither surprised nor disgusted when I relate that that afternoon saw us entering the rocky portals of the Wehra Thal, comfortably installed in a carriage which the Kurhaus at Todtmoos had sent down for our convenience. Well, our luggage had to go up somehow, and it seemed a pity not to accompany it; and if some one argues that the luggage might have gone up in the luggage cart, I only retort that

a tactful person would ignore the fact, and let us enjoy our 16 marks' worth of extravagance with an easy conscience. At any rate, we consoled ourselves with the marked absence of pedestrians on the road, and our consolation increased when, after three hours' steady uphill driving, our destination, Todtmoos, appeared in sight. During these three hours we had ample opportunity to admire the unique qualities and beauties of the Wehra Thal. I say unique, for there is no other valley in the Black Forest which offers the same unbroken loneliness, and whose road, cut in places in the very face of the rock, has been won with so much skill and difficulty. From the moment that we left the ruins of the Castle Bärenfels behind us to the moment when Todtmoos-Au first broke the monotony—a matter of two hours' driving—there was no vestige of human habitation on either side of the rocky heights which bind in the river, and in the valley itself there is no room for anything save the magnificently constructed road and the Wehra itself. It is a region of absolute loneliness, and yet, shut in as it is, it is not oppressive. The immense precipices on either side are crowned with the richest foliage, the torrent thundering towards the plains is of silver clearness, the ferns and wild flowers grow in luxuriant profusion along the wayside, and the winding road, which at one point crosses from the right bank to the left, bears the traveller with rapid alternation from shadow to sunshine. Save for the absence of human life there is no monotony here, and to my mind the stretch from Wehr to Todtmoos is one of the most perfect specimens of typical Black Forest scenery; there is grandeur without oppressiveness, a splendid beauty warmed and softened by the green of the firs and beeches which grow, as it seems, on the very face of the rock, a charm half-pastoral, half-romantic, an atmosphere which seems to have sunk from the regions of sunshine above to the valley shadows, warm and yet full of a vigorous freshness. But to begin at the beginning! Half an hour after we had left the village of Wehr behind us we reached the entrance to the gorge—for from this point it is more gorge than valley—and saw above us the ruins of Bärenfels, perched on the summit of an inaccessible-looking precipice and half hidden by an overgrowth of trees and rough, tangled shrubs. The race of Barenfels seems to have been a hard-drinking one, and not over-popular amongst the down-trodden peasantry of their neighbourhood. At any rate, Kurt von Barenfels, surnamed the 'Lütplager,' or 'Peoples' Plague,' was condemned after his death to wander round the castle in the form

THE WEHRA.

of a great red hound, followed by savage dogs, presumably the spirits of his former victims. Beyond the ruins the road winds its way along the left bank under the rocky heights of the 'Hirschsprung' (Stag's Leap), a spot from which, so the story runs, a hunted stag sprang from one side of the valley to the other, and then over the so-called Sonnenbrucke (Sunbridge) to the right bank of the Wehra. At this point the beauty of the valley reaches its highest perfection, and we persuaded our sleepy Jehu to pull in his horses for a moment and allow us a longer view of the rough, picturesque bridge, the tunnelled roadway, the clear waters hurrying over their smooth bed of rock out of the shadow into the sunshine, and on either side the high prison walls with their crown of olive green mingled with the lighter, softer hues of silver beech. From thence onwards the character of the valley begins to change, and by the time the traveller reaches Todtmoos-Au he has left the wild deserted regions behind him and has entered into a broad stretch of pastoral land, dotted with sawmills and straw-roofed cottages. On the left a magnificent modern building drew our attention, and our driver informed us that it was the Sanatorium Wehrawald, the highest situated hospital for consumptives in Germany, and famous for the perfection of its organisation and accommodation. Five minutes later Todtmoos itself was heralded by a few strolling 'Kur' guests and the spire of the village church, and just as dusk was beginning to close in about us, and the air to become a trifle too keen for our summer attire, our carriage drew up with stylish smartness at the Kurhaus doors.

Our first impression of Todtmoos was curiously unlike the impression which any other Black Forest village or 'Bad' had made upon us. In a sense we were again in a 'popular' resort with hotels and a Kurhaus and even a Kur band, but the atmosphere and the very people were very different. It was as though the fresh mountain air had kept the society—or would-be society —folk down in the valley, or, at any rate, had blown away something of their society manners and customs.

As we wandered about the chief street that evening after supper we were strongly reminded of a Swiss mountain village, with its careless 'va et vien' of visitors, its little shops, its picturesque cottages, its brightly lighted inns and hotels, from whence come the sounds of music; only here the gaiety is a little less pronounced and less overshadowed by the stupendous presence of surrounding giants. As we lazily wended our way up the road which leads to the sanatorium we were conscious of a peaceful melancholy which seemed a very part, the very spirit of the village lying in the broad valley beneath. We seemed again 'at the top of the world,' and there was, in spite of the laughing Kur guests and the cheery scrapings of the string band, a certain atmosphere of loneliness and gravity about us. We felt as though the memory of winter with its snow and fierce hurricanes still haunted the mountains, the forest, and the people, and that we, too, could not wholly escape its solemn influence. We climbed higher, and gradually left the other wanderers behind us. The waltz melodies faded into silence and gave place to the distant tinkling of cow-bells. Involuntarily I thought of similar evenings at Zermatt and Chamonix, but though there was no tooth-like shadow of a Matterhorn, and no white cloud of a Mont Blanc to overawe me, there was impressivness enough in the solemn stretch of fir-covered forest. We stood upwards of half an hour watching the changing aspect in the little world at our feet. As night deepened, lights sprang up all over the valley, marking as though with a beacon the widely separated homesteads; the bell of the church, which stood protectingly above the village, tolled out the hour, and then, soon afterwards, the beacons went out upon the mountain-side, and in the broad sweep of the valley only a bevy of lights remained to tell that the pleasure-seeking guests were still awake ; but Todtmoos, the real Todtmoos, with its hard-working inhabitants, slept the sleep of the just.

The next morning, contrary to expectation, arrived with sunshine and a clear blue sky, so that we were early on foot, and having already some experience of Black Forest weather we determined to leave the near surroundings to a less propitious occasion and start off for Herrischried, a village situated in the valley of the Murg. The Murg Valley is one of the most interesting stretches of country in the Black Forest, and though our own rambles did not on this occasion lead us farther than Herrischried, a prolonged excursion to the ruins of Castle Wieladingen over Hollingen is strongly recommended to the rambler who has time and energy to spare. The walk to Herrischried took us two and a half hours, but as the road lay through leafy forest and gave us at its highest points a fine panorama of Todtmoos on the one hand and of the distant Alps on the other, the time passed with surprising swiftness, and only certain hungry cravings warned us that the dinner hour was at hand. Herrischried boasts of

HERRISCHRIED.

two inns, at both of which a good, if simple,
meal (with trout) can be obtained, and whilst
mine host of the 'Deutscher Kaiser' was preparing the latter dainty for us we amused
ourselves by wandering about the straggling
village and inspecting the churchyard. Any
rambler with a sufficient knowledge of the
German language and a sense of humour is
strongly advised never to pass a Black Forest
churchyard without a visit, for the lyrical
efforts of the village poet are often as delightful as they are bewildering in thought and
rhyme. But apart from the churchyard Herrischried has other interests to offer. Here, for
the first time, we came across the Black Forest
cottages of the old type, alas! becoming every
day more rare, and it was with the greatest
difficulty that my German friend was dragged
away from the picturesque thatched dwellings
which, later on in our rambles, we shall inspect
more closely. Fortunately trout offered here
even stronger attractions, so that we were
presently busy with knife and fork, at the same
time listening to mine host's account of his
village and its eventful history. It is always
with an effort that the traveller realises that
these quiet, 'sleepy little nests' have a history
at all, but Herrischried, unlikely though it
seems, has seen stirring times. Herrischried

is what one might call the capital of a whole union of villages which once bore the name of 'Hauensteiner Einung' (Hauenstein is the general name for the country about the Murg), and which possessed a freedom almost amounting to that of an independent state. But here again we find the interfering hand of two old acquaintances—the Count of Habsburg and the Abbot of St. Blasien. The former made Herrischried and the whole of the union his own, and it followed that in the course of time the tract of rugged country became Austrian. But the real troubles of the union began with the rise of St. Blasien to power, and the subsequent 'grabbing' which formed the earthly policy of the monastery's spiritual leaders. Against this policy the Hauensteiners had the bad taste to rise *en masse* during the Peasants' War, and from that time onwards there was a constant struggle between the two parties. At the beginning of the eighteenth century the St. Blasien authorities made an attempt to regain their power over the district, whereupon the so-called Saltpetre War broke out under the leadership of one Johann Albiez, a saltpetre boiler. The struggle was marked by the extraordinary fanaticism shown on both sides, and though the conduct of the religious party was sufficient to justify most things, the

Hauensteiners seem in many cases to have managed to go 'one better' in the matter of rapine and barbarous cruelty. The war was suppressed by Austria, but it broke out twice again, the last time in 1815. The Thirty Years' War, however, had somewhat damped the fighting spirits of the unruly peasants, whose homes for the most part had been laid in ruins, and the rising was of short duration. It is rather curious, seeing that their forefathers spent their lives in fighting clerical authority, that the Hauensteiners of to-day are a bigoted, superstitious race, wholly under the control of their priests, themselves often half-educated fanatics. For the rest the Hauensteiners, or Hozenwalder, as they are also called, on account of their short black trousers (Hozen-Hosen), are a peculiar and interesting people. There is Slavic blood in their veins, and this mingling with the original Alemannen element has brought about a peculiar and often contradictory character. The Hozenwalder of to-day is powerfully built, of dark complexion, capable of extreme brutality, but usually good-natured, obstinate, revengeful, and boastful, but delightfully witty when some special festivity has torn him out of his usual cautious reserve. He is fond of a wild kind of waltz, and dances with a passion which recalls his Slavic origin, and his folk-songs are for the most part of a serious, melancholy type.

As everywhere in the Black Forest, the Hauenstein region boasts of its own peculiar 'Tracht,' or national costume, and the rambler who wishes to see the peasant at his best should try to visit Herrischried on a Sunday, the one and only day when the 'Tracht' is taken out of the family wardrobe. Unfortunately this custom of wearing their historic dress (the Hauenstein Tracht dates from the fifteenth century) is fast dying out The peasants themselves have no idea of the beauty of their dress, and the spread of modern ideas, above all the vulgar and impertinent curiosity of tourists, who treat the peasants very much as though they were so many animals in masquerade, has helped to make the Tracht, at any rate in Hauenstein, a rare and, on weekdays, an unknown sight. Nevertheless the Hauenstein dress is one of the most peculiar and interesting of the many types which the Black Forest has to show. The men, besides their short black trousers, wear white stockings and black boots which reach half-way up the calf of the leg, a long full coat over a red vest, and a big-brimmed felt hat, or, if they are young and unmarried, small fur caps. The women's attire also varies in accordance with their age and position. The more elderly are, as a rule, dressed simply in black with full short skirts, a close-fitting head-dress, and red stockings. The girls, on the contrary, are as gay as peacocks in their red jackets, green aprons, blue skirts, coloured neck-trimmings, white stockings, and shoes with red strings. Their wonderfully long tresses of hair are tied in plaits with wide silk ribbons, on their heads they wear gold-embroidered caps —'Plunderkappen'—and around their waists a silver belt. Altogether, in spite of the mixture of colours, the costume is a handsome and expensive one. Perhaps the latter fact explains a little the gradual disappearance of the 'Tracht,' for a really 'full dress' outfit for a girl costs as much as a Paris model, as those who have tried to obtain one for carnival wear have discovered to their distress.

The day on which we visited Herrischried being a weekday, we saw nothing of all these wonders, but an old peasant allowed herself to be persuaded into showing us the contents of her wardrobe, so that we were able to admire the beautiful embroidered garments of her youth.

She appeared very much amused at our admiration, and in spite of our indignant protests she insisted that the modern attire of the more advanced village girls—consisting of cheap town hats and coats and skirts—was much finer.

RAMBLES IN THE BLACK FOREST

By the time we reached Todtmoos again our energy allowed us no more than a five minutes' pull up the steep hill which leads to the church —an interesting if ugly place of worship. Its foundation can be traced back to the beginning of all things as far as Todtmoos is concerned. About the middle of the thirteenth century a certain priest, Dietrich von Rickenbach, having in a dream received orders from the Virgin Mary, built a chapel in her honour in a region which was called Todtmoos on account of the — then — dangerous condition of the ground. The miracles performed on the holy spot drew the attention of Rudolf of Habsburg and eventually of the Pope himself, who having blessed it with numberless 'pardons' created it a place of pilgrimage 'première ordre.' And a place of pilgrimage it is to-day, as the 'stations' which line the road from St. Blasien, together with the numberless gifts and votives, testify. At the time of our visit a pilgrimage had just taken place, and the whole street was gaudily decorated with arches of imitation flowers and pines. On the two sides of the hill on which the church stands, wooden booths had been opened for the sale of holy pictures and rosaries—also other less spiritual things. On the whole, the actual inhabitants of Todtmoos seemed to take these pilgrimages with an in-

TODTMOOS.

difference faintly touched with scepticism, but there was no doubt as to the devoutness of the pilgrims themselves.

We had not finished our exploration of the church before a sudden thunder-storm put an end to any further plans for that day, and we were compelled to retire to the comfortable Kurhaus reading-rooms, there to beguile ourselves with belated English newspapers and listen to the artillery firing that was going on about our heads. A thunder-storm in the valley is child's play compared to the upheaval of the elements which the Black Forest mountains witness so often. One feels as though one were at the very heart of the commotion, and to witness the storm from a mountain-top is a wonderful and terrific experience, not wholly unmixed with danger, as the seared and broken pine trees bear testimony. Unfortunately a storm must be paid for with an almost certain if only temporary break in the weather, so that we were not surprised the next morning to find the sky already dotted with those 'cotton-wool' clouds whose presence bodes ill for the day. Consequently we refrained from wandering far afield and contented ourselves with Todtmoos' direct surroundings Naturally we discovered a waterfall—two waterfalls even, the one situated in a charming little ravine about ten minutes' walk from the hotel world. The Rabenschlucht (Raven's Gorge), as it is called, is one of the most delightful miniature gorges that I have met in the Black Forest. All that is awe-inspiring and terrific in the rocky valleys we have already seen is here translated into a child's plaything; minute boulders, tremendous 'falls' of two feet high, and breakneck paths and bridges across the breadth of the foaming torrent delight the wanderer's eye, and though I am afraid we allowed ourselves a disrespectful laugh at the waterfall's most tremendous 'effect'—a cascade over a high boulder—we lengthened the ten minutes' necessary for the whole walk into half an hour, lingering by the prettiest points and attempting to take photographs which, I regret to say, came out looking like pictures of a damp sheet hung out to dry. From thence our way took us along to *the* waterfall, this time a genuine concern which evidently felt itself vastly superior to any toy-gorge, and was, perhaps on that account, not quite so successful. Still, it looked pleasantly cool and sparkling as it came tumbling down from the rocks above into the silvery brook, and the walk at the top which leads back to Todtmoos, past interesting peasants' farms, or 'Höfe,' as they are called, is well worth the trouble and

ST. ANTONI.

does not tax the powers of even the weariest rambler.

As we strolled back to the hotel, a noticeable change in the atmosphere and a clearing of the sky told us that the south-west wind had shifted to the north, so that we had the right to count on fine weather. Thus that afternoon, our 'wander-lust' still being strong on us, we set off for a purposeless ramble along the beautiful paths which lead upwards into the forest. Without any particular reason we obeyed the behests of the signposts pointing to St. Antoni, and to them we owe one of our pleasantest walks. Not that St. Antoni, a little chapel on the hillside, offered any particular attraction, but the afternoon light, deepening gradually to evening, seemed to transform the whole forest into fairyland. In no other country of my travels have I witnessed such wonderful changes in colouring as in the Black Forest towards sunset; each moment brings a deeper tint, a new colour, and far back between the silver and purple stems there is a glimmer of fiery sunshine which recalls the glow in *Siegfried.* As evening advances the light seems to become almost threatening, the trunks of the firs and beeches, which rise like pillars towards the sky, turn from the softest rose to purple, the very green of the trees, the fresh, vivid green of spring is brilliant, fiery as though from inward illumination. Here and there a rivulet, creeping its way through the ferns and mosses, catches a last ray of the sun before it tumbles in ghostly grey cascades towards the valley, and save for its mysterious bubbling song there is an unbroken silence. And so night comes on, the distant glow turns from red to mauve, and then dies into complete darkness ; the voice of the unseen water seems to grow louder, and among the trees some night-bird, startled by the belated rambler, flutters up out of reach of danger. The perfume of the pine and newly cut wood, lying piled up along the roadside, is borne on the calm air which the departed sun has warmed and softened, and the traveller, as he breaks out once more into the open country, feels that he has been in an enchanted world. It is, above all, a German world, as my German friend carefully explained to me on our way homewards from St. Antoni, and I felt that she was right, though I did not admit it. Whether one wishes them to or not, all the heroes of Germanic mythology rise up before one's eyes on such an evening as I have attempted to describe. The Black Forest, one is sure, must have been Siegfried's home, must have seen Wotan's earthly wanderings, and burnt in the glow of Loge's fiery embrace. It

COTTAGES NEAR TODTMOOS.

is a region full of the German spirit of romance
and legend, and it is for that reason, perhaps,
that the Black Forest is best known and
certainly best loved by the Germans themselves.

But to return to more substantial matters!
Our rambles on the following day took us far
afield, namely, to Schweigmatt over the village
of Gersbach. Once again I have to confess that
the journey was not performed on foot, for the
very sufficient reason, already once given, that
our luggage had to be conveyed per carriage,
and that there was no object in our not taking
the same advantage. Thus, as there was no
particular need for an early start, we made our
farewell to Todtmoos from the summit of the
Hochkopf (3600 feet), whence, too, we obtained
a fine view over to the Alps. The walk was
mostly over open ground, so that we were glad
that the sun had not as yet made up his
mind to put in an appearance. On the way
we passed a tiny little white-washed chapel,
whose bell an old peasant woman was busily
tolling. She informed us that she acted as bell-
man twice a day, once at eleven and once in the
evening, and generally, as it appeared, took the
place of the priest himself. Down in the valley
we had noticed that some of the more important-
looking peasants' homes were built with a small
belfry, and she told us that at the evening hour

the bell rang to call together all the members of the household for evening prayer, read by the chief Bauer (peasant) himself. As only old and wealthy families follow this custom, it is safe to look upon these belfries as a sign of wealth and 'blood.' Bidding our kindly informant farewell we returned to our hotel, there to find our carriage waiting and our boxes strapped in their places, and ten minutes later we looked back for a last time at Todtmoos before the forest hid it from our sight.

CHAPTER VIII

SCHWEIGMATT, THROUGH THE WIESE VALLEY, TO BADENWEILER

WE had chosen Schweigmatt (2550 feet) for our next stopping-place, for two reasons : the first reason was of a sentimental character and concerned a previous visit, made some years before, when I had caught a first glimpse of the Black Forest; the second, more practical, was that Schweigmatt formed a good starting-point for our wanderings up the valley of the Wiese. Our road lay through shady avenues as far as the village of Gersbach, where we stopped for half an hour to reconnoitre and excite the natives with our camera. I suppose there are few villages in the Black Forest so entirely unspoilt, so entirely the home of the natives themselves as this little straggling Gersbach. There is no hotel worthy of the name, only two inns, which appear to exist solely for the use of the villagers, and save for a few artists the place knows few visitors. Yet the rambler

who wishes to see something of the human
element in the Black Forest could not do
better than spend an hour or two in the rough,
uneven street which leads downhill between two
rows of picturesque, and consequently tumble-
down, cottages. As far as we could judge there
were no 'Grossbauer' (rich peasants) amongst
the inhabitants. the cottages, although typical,
were not of the type which we shall meet
later on, where the picturesqueness is obtained
—unconsciously, it is true—by a graceful structure and a lavish display of oak blackened by
the rain and sunshine of many scores of years.
These peasants' houses might often arouse the
envy of a rich man on the search for a summer
residence, but here in Gersbach the interest is
the interest of decay and ruin. True, the decay
and ruin is probably more apparent than real,
and the traveller, in judging the wealth or
poverty of a village in South Germany, must
always bear in mind that the German peasant is
absolutely indifferent to physical comfort and
appearances generally. As long as he has a roof
over his head and enough to eat, no matter
what, his needs are satisfied. Thus in Gersbach
the roofs are kept well thatched, but the doors
fall from their hinges, the steps which lead up to
the wooden balcony under the eaves are rotten,
the windows roughly patched and uncurtained.

GERSBACH.

Pigs and feathered folk of all kinds wander about the streets and mingle in amicable companionship with the bare-headed, bare-footed children, and every here and there some toothless old dame, clad in the poorest garb, peers out into the sunlit, sleepy street. There is dust, disorder, and poverty everywhere —at first sight—and though it undoubtedly offers irresistible attractions to the artistic eye, the English traveller, with the memory of spruce, built-by-the-dozen English cottages and elegantly clad English country maidens, will shake his head in pity for the 'miserable German peasant.' Unless he is unusually clear-sighted he will not see that the dust lies only where it can do no harm, that the disorder is almost calculated and never ventures into the homes themselves, that the apparent poverty is in reality merely the expression of an extreme frugality, and that the chances are that the toothless, withered old lady whose fate has aroused his contemptuous sympathy is probably far better off than many a well-to-do English yeoman's wife. Later on, when we left the village behind us and drove over the open stretch of country which leads to Schweigmatt, we had a further insight into the real conditions of the people. All along the road we met ox-wagons heavily laden with the first hay (the Black Forest peasant goes haymaking four times a year), and the sturdy teams, the sunburnt, handsome faces of the well-set-up figures of their drivers, the rosy-cheeked women, with their white kerchiefs tied over their hair, who smiled and nodded to us from the fields, did not suggest either misery or poverty. Undoubtedly the life they lead is a hard, strenuous one, and the women, who take their share with the men, age quickly, but the roughness of their lives and the comfortlessness of their homes is of their own choosing. They have not yet been educated to demand or expect luxury; they are primitive in their ways and tastes, and, for their country's sake, long may they remain so!

Half an hour's drive brought us once more into the forest. We were now in a region almost untrodden by the rambler's foot, and rarely used as a carriage-way, if one might judge by the narrow, grass-grown road, and we congratulated ourselves warmly on a cross-country route which took us so successfully from the vulgar throng. Save for the peasants, we had not met a single other traveller on the road, and the fact gave us, I fear, an unchristian-like satisfaction. Truth to tell, Schweigmatt is itself an out-of-the-way place, little known to the ordinary tourist, and a treasured secret of the German in search of absolute peace and

OX WAGON AT GERSBACH.

quiet. The Kurhaus, the only hotel and the only building for miles around, save for one or two peasants' cottages, is beautifully situated a few hundred feet below the tower of the Hohen Móhr, on the very borders of the forest, but with a magnificent uninterrupted panorama southwards over the Rhine to the Alps. The air is extraordinarily pure and bracing, even for the Black Forest, and the surrounding country beautiful enough to account for the crowded table d'hôte which greeted us on our arrival. The custom of forcing their guests to sit together at one long table is the one thing which annoys me in the conduct of the otherwise unimpeachable Black Forest *hôteliers*. Of course as their servants are few, and for the most part not very highly trained peasant girls, the business of serving is no doubt simplified by this method, and I know that the Germans themselves, being a more sociable people, prefer it, but I confess that my English soul invariably pants for the quiet and solitude of a separate table. I should add that a separate table can usually be obtained — for an extra charge. And the extra charge is just the rub, for though the original ' pension ' may be low enough there are always enough extras to make the bill rise considerably, especially, as in our case, where a simple night's stay does not

entitle the visitor to 'pension' terms. Thus
we condescended to take our places with the
rest, and Providence as a reward sent us a
'Bäuerin' in full 'Tracht' as a neighbour,
and her conversation—I think it was the first
time she had ever been in a hotel—recompensed
us entirely for other disadvantages.

Towards evening we wandered up the easy
path which leads to the Hohen Mohr, and on
the way a stray butterfly of fine dimensions
reminded me of my first experiences in the art
of butterfly collecting. Schweigmatt's protected
position, the wide stretches of sunlit meadow
which lie at the edge of the forest and cover
the hillside seem to favour the development of
the finest specimens, and I advise the collector
—but I prefer not to advise him. I should not
like to do my friend of the pale blue wings
such a bad turn. From the top of the tower
of Hohen Mohr we were able to obtain a full
view over the Alps before evening, and when
night came on and the full moon rose over the
Rhine Valley, it seemed to us that from where
we sat on the Kurhaus terrace we could still
see the ghostly outline of the snow-capped
mountains. The following morning we gave
our luggage into the hands of the host, with
the request that it should be registered to
Todtnau, whilst we ourselves took the footpath

down to the station Hausen-Raitbach in the valley of the Wiese. A little less than an hour's downhill walking brought us to our destination, and having time to spare we wandered over to Hausen, famous as the birthplace of Johann Peter Hebel, the greatest poet of the Black Forest. A tumble-down cottage next the inn 'zum Adler' bears the inscription 'Hebel's Heimat,' and it is curious to compare this humble, poverty-stricken beginning with the proud monument in the churchyard which tells the passer-by that 'Johann Peter Hebel, Baden's first prelate and sweet singer,' has found his rest in the quiet of his native village.

During our idle wanderings through Hausen's sleepy streets we were fortunate enough to meet a bevy of red-cheeked Black Forest maidens, decked in their best 'Tracht' and evidently bound on a day's excursion to some neighbouring town. Their costume reminded us that we had left the Hauensteiners far behind us, and that we were in the Markgraflerland—the land of wine, pretty girls, and quaint dress. Hausen is a Protestant village, consequently the 'Tracht' is also Protestant. In contrast to their Catholic sisters, who wear red, the Protestant women wear white kerchiefs over their heads whilst working in the fields, and on 'best days' they are distinguished by a wondrous and, to my mind, charming head-dress of broad, black silk ribbons, tied so as to form two big wings. The rest of the dress is very simple—a black dress with a shawl of black or white lace, crossed gracefully across the breast, being the usual garb —and its very simplicity, in comparison with the gorgeousness of some of the costumes, adds to its charm. Altogether the Markgrafler folk are remarkable for their honesty, simplicity, and straightforwardness, and these characteristics seem to find an expression in their dress and whole appearance.

From Hausen to the most important station on the Wiesen Thal line, Zell, the scenery offered us was of no particular beauty, but from Zell onwards the valley closed in and the mountains on either side rose up in a majesty which reminded us that we were nearing the great Feldberg and that these were his forerunners. North of the comparatively modern town Zell, the birthplace, by the way, of Weber's parents, we saw the rounded heights of the 'Zeller Blauen,' and every here and there a stream hurrying down from the mountains revealed to us the presence of the small but charming valleys which branch off to the right and left from the Wiese. Thus alternately narrowing and widening out again into peaceful meadow-land, but always accompanied by the range of mountains on

either side, the Wiese brought us to Schönau,
the chief town of the valley. Here, with the
help of our time-table, we had arranged for a
two hours' halt for lunch and a general survey
of the friendly overgrown village. In spite
of the fact that Schonau is chief town from the
official point of view, it has remained an old-
world place, and the green pastures which surround it justify fully the name it bears. For
the ending 'Au,' which we shall often meet
in this region, signifies 'meadow,' and the
adjective 'Schon' seems to have been chosen
to emphasise the superiority of the town over
its neighbours, 'Schlechtau' and 'Todtnau.'
Be it as it may, we were well pleased to endorse
the self-laudatory adjective, and our two hours'
stay was marked by an excellent, much-needed
meal at the 'Gasthaus zum Ochsen' and a
pleasant walk to 'Schonenbuchen,' a hamlet with
a chapel dedicated to St. Peter and famous in
the neighbourhood as a place of pilgrimage. A
decidedly curious picture represents the 'great'
battle of Schonenbuchen, though when and
against whom the battle was fought no one
seems to know. All that is certain is, that at
the critical moment when the inhabitants of
Schönenbuchen were obviously getting the worst
of the encounter, an army of angels—dressed
appropriately in Black Forest 'Tracht'—came

to the rescue by throwing sharp-pointed iron nails amongst the horses of the enemy, whereupon the latter, enraged by this proceeding, began to fight among themselves, the conflict ending so disastrously that the meadows ran with their blood down to the very banks of the Rhine. From this account it will be clear to the dullest and least appreciative rambler that Schönenbuchen and its inhabitants are certainly Heaven blessed. Altogether Schönau and the surrounding neighbourhood have seen hard struggles, for it was here that the Reformation began its passage through the Black Forest, and St. Blasien, who, as usual, had taken possession of the place, lost no time in crushing out the new teaching with a violence and cruelty which would have been the envy of the Spanish Inquisition. Nevertheless, in spite of all efforts on the part of the clerical party, the greater part of the Wiesen Valley became Protestant and has remained Protestant to this day.

Once more the train carried us northwards to the head of the valley and our destination Todtnau, and having retrieved our luggage we deposited ourselves at the friendly 'Gasthaus zum Ochsen' for the night. We were now in the very heart of the Black Forest mountains; like a toy-town that has somehow or other fallen into the hands of giants, Todtnau lies at the foot of the great, for the most part barren, monsters which tower up crushingly on either hand. Most magnificent of all is the view from the north-east side of the town, at the entrance of the Brandenburg Valley, which later offers itself as a route up to the Feldberg itself. But we had already made up our minds on the subject of the Feldberg. The sight of these new lands to conquer had aroused our ambition and enthusiasm to the highest pitch, and we did what we had never done before—we bought a knapsack; we crammed it to bursting-point with all the articles which civilisation has dubbed 'pure necessities,' entrusted our remaining belongings to our host, and turning our faces courageously northwards proceeded to attack the giant of the Black Forest *via* Todtnauberg and the inevitable waterfall. Now, a knapsack is a curious and treacherous thing. The first sight of its round, compact exterior fills you with a certain satisfaction; you marvel at the quantities which you have managed to crush into its limits and at the extraordinary lightness of the whole concern. Then you strap it on your back and march triumphantly through the town with your head high, with the knowledge that you are on adventure bent, that you are really 'roughing it,' that you are altogether a superior individual to that 'bloated aristocrat' lolling in her carriage and pair on the way from Boll to St. Blasien. Your step is still jaunty as you attack the first rise, but after ten minutes your cheery conversation flags; you begin to display a peculiar interest in the view, you fidget with the straps, which are beginning to cut unpleasantly into your shoulders, and dark suspicions that at the last moment your companion may have surreptitiously added to your burden begin to flit across your mind. After that your temper loses itself with a rapidity and completeness dependent on your own particular temperament and powers of self-control.

I was thankful when, after an hour and a half's groaning under my self-imposed burden, the hotel of Todtnauberg came in sight and set me free. Whilst awaiting our dinner—if I seem to mention meals more often than may appear necessary to a spiritually minded rambler, it is because they form such an agreeable break, and because one becomes painfully material in the strong, pure air—we inspected *the* waterfall, which, thanks to the recent rains, was in its most flourishing condition. The idea of describing waterfalls becomes odious in the Black Forest, where one meets the same type at almost every stopping-place, but I cannot pass this particular specimen without a word of recommendation. About three hundred feet in height the full torrent breaks over half a dozen smaller falls and finally throws itself *en masse* down a perpendicular precipice of rock. The finest view can be obtained from the bridge about a quarter of an hour from Todtnauberg, and thither therefore we repaired to fight the temptation to take obviously impossible photographs. With the afternoon came the hardest but also the most richly rewarded endeavours. Our way from the Todtnauberg brought us at first a fine view over the Alps, and later on a shady road through forest, until at last we gained the chief 'Hohenweg.' (The Hohenwege in the Black Forest are the well-kept roads which keep to the heights. It is possible to go from Basel to Karlsruhe entirely on these roads, which bear different numbers and are usually marked red on the maps.) At about the same moment as I had come to the decision that knapsacks were an invention of the powers of darkness for the discomfort and torture of an unsuspicious mankind, the Feldberger Thurm came in sight, and in spite of the fact that we were now on open ground and at the mercy of the sunshine, our courage revived and we struggled on heroically. On the whole we had all reason to be grateful for the sunshine, which, as every traveller of the Feldberg knows, can be only too easily replaced by terrific storms, or, what is worse, a dense, misleading mist. Whatever bad weather may happen to be lurking in the neighbourhood breaks over the Feldberg, and even those who know its paths well hesitate to move during one of the mists, knowing that he will either waste his time wandering in a circle or lose himself hopelessly in the marshy ground from whence the rivers of the Wiese and the Gutach take their source. This 'Feldberg Geist' (Spirit) has always been a much-feared guest, and the monks of St. Blasien, once more on the look out for something fresh to lay hold of, determined to exorcise the evil spirit and confine it to the limits of a holy battle. They therefore lit a fire by which they hoped to discover him, but unfortunately—or fortunately—he proved one too much for the hitherto unsubdued priests; appearing to them as a terrific storm spirit, he blew out their light, and, leaving them in pitch darkness, drove them helter-skelter down the mountain-side amidst hailstones and other unpleasantness. So the Feldberg Geist remained unconquered, and in spite of his interesting and mysterious 'past' we were grateful not to make his acquaintance. We were fortunate, too, in the view, which is rarely clear in summer, and from where we stood at the foot of the 'Luisen

Tower,' as it is called, we could see not only over the full length of the Feldberg and the neighbouring mountains, but far beyond, northwards over the Black Forest to the Hornisgrinde, westwards to the Vosges, and southwards the long chain of Alps to Mont Blanc itself. But all this splendour is a rarity, and the rambler who wishes to make its acquaintance must come in winter, when sport and magnificent scenery should amply recompense him for the time he will probably have to wait before the whole panorama reveals itself to him. As to the Feldberg itself, it represents a long, narrow plateau, running from east to west and marked by three distinct points. Our point of arrival, the so-called ' Hochste,' measures 4485 feet and boasts not only a tower but also a Gasthaus (zum Feldberg Thurm), to which latter place we at once repaired in order to rid myself of my Old-Man-of-the-Sea. Thus relieved I consented to explore the regions as far as the Seebuch, whose Bismarck Monument marks the most easterly point (4350 feet). On all sides the descent from the Feldberg plateau into the valleys is extremely steep, but here we looked down into what seemed a yawning abyss. Evening was already creeping up the mountain-sides, and it was only as a dim yet indescribably threatening shadow that we could see the Feldsee (lake) lying immediately (900 feet) below us. It was a curious, almost awe-inspiring, change to turn from the west, with its brilliant red glory, to the sombre chasm which at no time, not even in days of brightest sunshine, loses its character of melancholy and mystery. Surrounded two-thirds by rock and precipice and for the rest by ragged, storm-beaten pines the lake offers the wanderer a vision of wild, romantic scenery which has no rival in the Black Forest, and which seems, indeed, to belong to another world, a world of phantoms and untamable demons. In hours of storm the ghostly huntsman of the Feldberg rides on the back of the howling tempest over the lake, with a horde of skeleton followers at his heels, and the black waters light up for an instant with the flash of unearthly fire. And in other hours, when a sullen calm rests over the loneliness, the stems of fallen pine trees rise up out of the depths. The ground is covered with the wreckage of the storms, and ghostly shadows flit silently over the black waters. Even at evening, when only a dim outline was discernible, the fascination of the place was so strong over us that we lingered longer than was wise, and with the lights of our Gasthaus as guides we had to make our way back as best we could through the treacherous dusk. The reader will admit after this account that our rambles on that day were of a very genuine character, and will sympathise when I relate that we followed Mark Twain's example and missed the sunrise the next morning. Only, unlike him, we did it consciously and on purpose, which is, I suppose, scarcely a mitigating circumstance. Still, with the knowledge that we had a good walk before us, and that the knapsack was on no account to be forgotten, we felt justified in a late breakfast, which was early enough, however, to allow us the full enjoyment of the wonderful fresh morning air and a view over the Black Forest to a horizon still pink from the last glow of what must have been—I speak under the influence of a pure supposition—a magnificent sunrise.

Leaving the third point of the Feldberg—the Baldenwegerbuck—to the north, we proceeded on our way downwards to the Feldbergerhof, a large and comfortable hotel, about an hour's walk from our own quarters of the previous night. As we walked, the full significance of the name 'Feldberg' (Field Mountain) was brought home to us. The numerous little huts, inhabited during the summer only, the stray cattle which crossed our path, the unshaded stretch of grassy land which reaches half - way down the mountain - side, reminded us of a Swiss pasture, and we were

137

not sorry to regain the shade of the forest. Save for the intrepid mountain ash, which here and there has managed to obtain a foothold on the precipitous south side, and a short, stubbly grass, the Feldberg is without vegetation, and after rain the ground becomes a swamp, from whence the Wiese and our old friend the Gutach-Wutach take their source.

It is hardly necessary to mention that the Feldberg once belonged to the monastery of St. Blasien; to-day the Feldbergerhof and the woods on the east side are the property of the Furst of Fürstenberg, who has his chief residence at Donaueschingen.

For our return journey we had determined to take the Wiese itself as our guide, and having tracked the river to its source, a quarter of an hour's walk from the hotel 'Feldberg,' we paused to take breath—our descents are as violent as our ascents are 'gemütlich' — and admire the grand, rocky surroundings with which the Wiese has chosen to frame the place of its birth. From thenceward, following the orders of the faithful signpost, we entered into the beautiful Hebelweg which leads through the gorge into the Branderberger Valley. Countless little waterfalls came scampering down from the heights to join the river, and incidentally, I suppose, to amuse the wanderer, who must cross the Wiese no less

138

than eleven times by means of rustic bridges before he reaches the high-road again. Personally, I found waterfalls and bridges alike a constant source of interest, and I suspect my companion of taking a childish pleasure in standing on the middle of the latter and throwing branches of fallen trees into the hurrying water in order to race them to the next point. Altogether I have noticed, for some unknown reason, running water makes children of us all, and it is wonderful how much more pleasantly the time slips past when one has a brook or a river for a companion on one's rambles. Hence the hour and a half which we needed to reach the Fahl seemed but half that time, and we faced the next hour and a half on the high-road through the fine Branderberger Valley with all good courage, and reached our headquarters at Todtnau with the feeling that our adventurous ramble with the knapsack—if sometimes painful — had at least given us a splendid glimpse of the Feldberg and of the great group of mountains which acknowledge it lord. At any rate, we were now in full training, and in spite of our recent exertions we occupied the rest of the day by strolling along the wooded paths which lead upwards from the valley, notably to the Hebelshöhe, a delightful spot from which the wanderer can obtain a fine view over Todtnau.

This ended our stay in the region of the Wiese Valley. Having obtained the advice and assistance of our host, and made considerable use of his telephone, we proceeded the next morning with the train back to Schonau, where, according to our arrangements, a carriage and pair waited to take us across country to Baden-weiler. As the reader will perceive, therefore, our rambles, from the pedestrian point of view, were temporarily at an end; and I confess that the change from the weary, knapsack-burdened wanderer of the day before, to the lady of ease and luxury reclining in her hired victoria, was a wholly agreeable one. Moreover, it was a cheap drive—a positive economy—for, had we gone by rail our way would have taken us over a long, expensive, zigzag route, and walking was obviously impossible. After all, there comes a moment when the most patient worm turns, and though I had borne a knapsack without complaint (at least without *much* complaint), I should have turned most decidedly at the thought of the contents of our good-sized portmanteau. All this is said in case the reader should suspect us of laziness or wanton extravagance.

Our road led for the first part through fairly open country, mounting steadily as we approached the region of the Belchen (3245 feet) and the

Kòlhgarten. The former mountain, which we admired from a distance only, is the third highest in the Black Forest, and its abrupt rise and isolated position make it by far the most imposing. The Feldberg's plateau-like summit detracts from its height, the pointed peak of the Belchen lends it apparently the 240 feet which it in reality requires to make it the Feldberg's equal. The view from the summit is, if anything, more picturesque and extensive; but we had had enough of views and mountain-climbing for the time being, and having enjoyed trout at the pleasant little inn of Neuenweg, we continued on our way upward over the rounded hills and past wide stretches of rich pasture-land. Then, as always in the Black Forest, no sooner had our sturdy horses dragged us and our luggage to the highest point than our way led down once more in sweeping curves through a forest of pine and fir. Another half-hour and the first villas of Badenweiler came into view, abruptly reminding us that we had left the primitive regions of the Black Forest behind us, and had returned to a world of ancient and modern culture.

CHAPTER IX

BADENWEILER AND FREIBURG

' WHEN in Rome do as the Romans do' is a good
motto to take with one when travelling, and
since of our own free will we had chosen to
turn our back on simplicity in order to see
something of the most luxurious Black Forest
life, we determined to do the thing in the style
proper to Badenweiler, and, scorning the offers
of smaller hotels, deposited ourselves and our
belongings at the famous Römer Bad. And my
advice to the traveller following our route is—
go and do likewise, for it can be truly said of
most Black Forest hotels that the most expensive
is usually the cheapest. At any rate, the
difference in price between one hotel and another
is ridiculously small in comparison with the re-
finements and luxuries which are offered for the
little extra expense. The truth of the matter
is that the smaller hotels are not really rougher
on account of the lower terms ; their cuisine,
serving, and accommodation are arranged to suit

142

the style of a certain class of people—people for the most part who look upon delicate food and dressing for dinner with an unappreciative eye. *Bien entendu* I speak only of such places as Badenweiler, where the hotels are all more or less pretentious. In little village places no one need fear accepting the low terms offered—that is to say, if they can be content with simple fare—but in towns it is always wiser to add one or two marks to the daily expense, and avoid the 'cheap' boarding-houses and family hotels, which in reality are only cheap in an unpleasant sense of the word. Moreover, in this particular instance the Hotel Romer Bad is an essential part of Badenweiler. It is like the Insel Hotel in Constance—not to have stayed in it is to have missed a chief feature of the place ; and for the rambler who has been existing on the contents of a knapsack it is a rare delight to unpack in an elegant bedroom, adorn himself in his best clothes, and dine amidst the glitter and splendour of a really fashionable world. For Badenweiler is not a St. Blasien ; its fine folk are really fine folk—at any rate, as far as wealth is concerned—and the German bourgeois element trying to be smart and up-to-date, and failing, utterly sinks into the background. I confess that that evening, as we entered the beautiful dining-room, I felt for the first time ashamed of

143

sunburnt hands and face ; I had hitherto been
rather proud of them, but our elegant neighbours,
who obviously never ventured out without the
protection of a parasol, made me feel a very
uncouth person—a sort of country cousin who
has wandered into superior regions by mistake.
Still, the first evening in the Black Forest's
second great watering-place was both pleasant
and refreshing, and prepared us for our tour of
inspection on the following day.

I have spoken of Badenweiler as the second
great watering-place not on account of the
inferiority of its natural charms, but because
as a fashionable residence, as a social resort, it
stands no comparison with Baden-Baden in the
eyes of the society world. Everything, though
elegant, is on a smaller, quieter scale ; the
numberless private villas which lie on the
outskirts of the town denote the existence of
a wealthy class, who come to enjoy a peaceful
home-life, and the whole ‘Kur’ life bears the
same somewhat subdued stamp. At no time
does Badenweiler produce the same, not
altogether admirable, class of visitors which
assemble in Baden-Baden in the great race
week, and the forms of entertainment offered
are scarcely exciting. In a word, the world
which favours Badenweiler is a fashionable
world, but a world in search of health, of quiet

KURGARTEN, BADENWEILER.

with beautiful surroundings and a certain outspoken elegance and refinement. The verb *s'amuser* is not the only verb in Badenweiler, and this fact marks the great difference between it and its sister, Baden-Baden.

As for Badenweiler itself, apart from its hotels and its visitors, it is rather difficult to discover where it is and of what it consists. When the exodus sets in, nothing remains but a handful of natives and a few melancholy shops, but the wonderful climate of the place is inducing winter guests to put in an appearance, so that it is likely that in time to come Badenweiler will be as popular in winter as in summer. Protected by the high walls of the Blauen— sometimes called Hochblauen to distinguish it from the Zellblauen—Badenweiler (1266 feet) feels little of the rough winds that blow over other parts of the Black Forest, and her elevated position saves her from the damp mists which hang over the Rhine Valley beneath her. Thus invalids and travellers, returning from southern countries, are thankful to make Badenweiler a halting-place; but I must admit that after the mountain regions from which we had come we found it somewhat stifling and closed in, and on the first day our energies were only sufficient to drag us wearily round the sights of Badenweiler itself. In this respect Badenweiler has much to offer, for almost more than any other place in the Black Forest she bears the mark of history on her walls. Her ruined castle, above all the fragments of the great thermal baths built by her founders, the Romans, transport the modern visitor back through the centuries to another and perhaps greater civilisation. Our first wanderings led us through the pleasant Kurgarten—fortunately situated next our hotel—up a narrow winding path into the ruins, which overlook the Rhine Valley. There is no doubt that the massive walls stand on the foundations of one of the Roman watch-towers, which at one time ran in a long chain from north to south. The situation, allowing for an uninterrupted view of the Rhine and the Vosges, and guarded on all other sides by forest and mountain, must have appealed irresistibly to the Roman military eye, and in the future ages the Germanic successors were no less quick to perceive the advantages of such a place of defence. The history of the castle from that time onwards is a chequered one. At first the residence of one of the Zähringer counts, who called the whole region round it Badenweiler, to distinguish it from the Castle Baden in the Oos Valley (Weiler signifies hamlet), it passed in succession into the hands of the counts of Freiburg, Strassburg, and Hochberg, eventually returning to the family of the original possessors. The present Grand Duke of Baden, who is a member of the Zahringer house, has also made Badenweiler a favourite autumn residence, though—as is easily understood—the decidedly draughty and inhospitable halls of his fathers know him no more. The French, to whom the Black Forest owes most of her ruins, laid their devastating hands on the castle in 1678, and since then it has been allowed to sink into a picturesque decay. From the foot of the rising ground, on which the shattered walls still rest, the Kurgarten stretches down to the old Roman baths, and in spite of a tempting Kur band discoursing restful music at an agreeable distance from a comfortable nook, where I had seated myself to enjoy the view, I was miserably led away to new historical investigations. The large sum of 40 pfennig procured the entry to the enclosure which has been built round the baths, together with the guidance of a proud custodian. She pointed out to us the square pillar at the entrance which bears the clear inscription 'Dianae Abnob,' and informed us that the baths had been undoubtedly dedicated to that goddess, who *du reste* was looked upon as a patroness by the Romans garrisoned in these regions. Probably her love of the chase justly entitled her to the position. As for the baths

themselves, they were intensely interesting—
for people with a large supply of imagination.
An uninformed person would probably take them
for the remnants of a house which had been
pulled down some years back, and for unknown
reasons covered over with a zinc roofing. I do
not mean to be disrespectful—I merely mean
that the original marble splendour is a thing of
the long past. The outlines of the baths, the
resting, drying, and massaging rooms are fairly
clearly defined, though the pipes by which the
water was brought into the baths have not been
discovered. By their size it is presumed that
they were public baths which fell into disuse on
the arrival of the Alemannen, who neither
realised the healing powers of the springs,
nor, apparently, cared much for baths of any
sort.

Having duly inspected the carefully preserved
ruins, which date from the time of the Emperor
Hadrian, and conjured up pictures of the elegant
Romans, who in those days sought their health
and pleasure in the marble precincts, we continued our wanderings through the Kurgarten
and eventually chanced to enter the famous
Marmorbad (Marble Bath), erected in imitation
of the Roman model. It must be confessed that
the imitation is the more attractive, and the
neighbouring Markgrafenbad, which contains

every thinkable convenience and comfort, makes one desirous of spending one's days in the beautifully clear water. But such pleasant idleness is not for ramblers, whose time is, after all, subject to certain limitations ; and, moreover, that important function, dinner, recalled us to the hotel. The worst of hotels of the Romer Bad class is that they are conducive to a state of *dolce far niente*—especially after dinner— and it required a considerable amount of firm-ness and cajolery on the part of my German friend to bring me on the road down to Ober-weiler and from thence to the ruins of Castle Neuenfels. I think it must have been the gloomy history of the place which tempted us up to the crumbling walls, for few families have come to so tragic and mysterious an end as the family of Neuenfels, and probably few castles would have so much to relate if the power of speech were granted to them as this particular castle. Not that its early history offers much excitement. Unlike most of their neighbours, the Neuenfels were loved by their subjects and enjoyed the reputation of kind and considerate masters, so the tragedy which cut off the race seems the more terrible and inexplicable. The story, as it has been handed down, is that in 1540 the castle was inhabited by its old lord, Christoph von Neuenfels, his wife and daughter, and five serving people. The way down to the village being somewhat long and tedious, a large dog had been trained to go down to the village every day and bring back a supply of meat. Great was the surprise of the villagers, therefore, when one day the faithful animal failed to put in its customary appearance, and the surprise increased to alarm as the days passed and still nothing was heard of the inhabitants of the castle. At last a party of the more courageous spirits ventured up, and forcing a way into the inner courtyard found the Lord of Neuenfels and his whole household murdered. No trace of the murderers was ever found, and the crime remains a mystery to this day. But since then no one has dared to inhabit the gloomy rooms, and little by little decay has laid the haunted castle in ruins. We lingered some time in the solitude of the ivy-grown walls and allowed our imagination to run riot, painting the dread scene which they must have witnessed before they bade their farewell to their last inhabitants. Thus having reduced ourselves to a pleasant state of 'creepiness' we set out on the way home, this time choosing the path over the Schwartze saddle, from whence we had a fine view over Badenweiler, and so reached the Niederweiler. Our guide-book informed us that this walk is particularly to be recommended on

BADENWEILER AND FREIBURG

Sunday morning between ten and eleven o'clock, as the wanderer can then enjoy the sound of twelve different churches ringing their bells at the same time. Personally, I find one church bell more than enough, but should the reader have avaricious tastes in this matter I give him the information for what it is worth.

Once more in Badenweiler we were still sufficiently energetic after our three hours' walk to look into the Protestant church, which, though it has been rebuilt and presents from the outside an entirely modern appearance, contains some curious old relics from the original building. Amongst other matters of interest we discovered an ancient Gothic wall painting representing a 'Todentanz,' or 'danse Macabre,' probably the oldest painting of the kind in Germany. I said we 'discovered' it, which statement, I fear, is a distortion of the true facts of the case. It was actually discovered by the art-historian Wilhelm Lübke, some few years before, and when I mention ourselves in the matter I merely mean that we came across it without being led by the hand by a guide-book—the only form of discovery left to us ordinary mortals. We finished our day in the Kurgarten, listening to the band, which seemed literally to play morning, noon, and night, and flattered ourselves that our day's rambles had entitled us to the pleasure of a thoroughly luxurious evening.

On the whole Badenweiler is not conducive to serious pedestrian effort; the energies relax easily in the mild, somewhat enervating atmosphere, and one finds oneself only too inclined to indulge in what may be described as 'watering-place walks,' that is to say, placid saunterings along the paths laid out for the benefit of the fashionable and not very enterprising 'Kur' guests. Moreover, Badenweiler is essentially a place of small rambles; the woods lie so close to the hotel doors and are so temptingly beautiful that the most energetic begins to ask himself why he should bother to move on, or if he does decide to reach some particular point of interest, he usually finds that it has been placed by an obliging chance at half an hour's distance. Thus our next enterprising feat was performed by mistake— one might almost say against our will. We had wandered up to Hausbaden (1572 feet), a fine hotel situated well outside Badenweiler, for the benefit of those who wish for greater quiet and fresher air, and happening to follow the pleasant road which winds upwards in gentle gradations through the forest, we found ourselves after an hour confronted with a signpost bearing the inscription, 'To the Blauen—one hour.' After having conquered the Feldberg, it had not occurred to us to do any more mountain-climbing in this region, and personally I felt as though the signpost had played us a rather mean trick. But my German friend, who is Teutonically thorough, was quite determined.

"It is absurd to be so near and not go to the end," she declared. And thereafter came a long string of the Blauen's attractions, which, of course, decided matters, for by the time we had argued out the pros and cons the summit was within half an hour's walk, and the idea of a Gasthaus in such close proximity effectually silenced my protests. I do not like to own it, but for once the guide-book was in the right: the Blauen (3481 feet) *is* worth the trouble of getting there, and the trouble is minimised by the fact that, unlike the Feldberg, the paths which lead to the summit are shaded by thick forest almost to the hotel doors. All the more wonderful is the outlook from the tower which has been built close to the hotel. Eastwards the Belchen hides the Feldberg from the sight, but southwards, on a fine day, the whole Alpine range to Mont Blanc is visible, and northwards the spire of the Freiburger cathedral rises clearly against the horizon. Being, as usual, lucky in our weather, we had the benefit of the whole panorama, which included westwards, our old friends the Vosges; but it is very possible that other ramblers may be less fortunate. For the Blauen, which marks the extreme westerly frontier of the Black Forest, is the starting-point for all the worst storms. They break with terrific force against its summit, roll on to the Belchen and Feldberg, and from thence northwards over the whole forest. Well may the walls of the Gasthaus be strongly built and the windows reinforced by a double glass! For when the thunder crashes against the heights to the accompaniment of a howling tempest, it is as though the very gates of pandemonium have been thrown open, letting loose a million relentless demons who beat with savage unseen hands against every obstacle that ventures to obstruct their path. The mere chance of witnessing one of these mighty, awe-inspiring outbreaks would alone tempt me to make the Blauen a few days' resting-place, but apart from that—and, after all, the chance is a very doubtful one—the surroundings are beautiful enough to prevent the visitor from feeling the loneliness of the situation in anything but a pleasant degree. After the hot-house temperature of Badenweiler the wonderful cool, bracing air was like a cup of strong wine, and we knew that our 'wander-lust' had revived and that our hours in the land of luxury were consequently numbered. We had rejoiced to regain civilisation, but the civilisation of a fashionable watering-place is of a wearying kind, and our two hours' stay on the Blauen had taught us our own needs. We had done with the flesh-pots of Egypt, and the wilds reclaimed us. No sooner realised, than we bade the hospitable Blauen Gasthof farewell and turned homewards with the full intention of packing our possessions together in preparation for the next day's move. For our return way we followed the advice of our host and chose the path which leads over the rocks of the Alten Mann. I do not know why they are called after the 'Old Man,' unless the bald, rugged appearance of the region suggested the name to some imaginative person. Or, perhaps, the name has a diabolical significance. At any rate, the descent by the roughly cut steps, over rustic bridges and round by railed-in galleries, is picturesque and wild enough, though somehow the close neighbourhood of Badenweiler made us feel that the 'wildness' must be put on, and that the Alten Mann was in reality merely a rockery arranged for the amusement of the Kur guests. From thence to the Sophien Ruh was only a short quarter of an hour, but the Sophien Ruh, though it offers a pleasant outlook towards the Rhine, had small attraction after the Blauen panorama. Moreover, the very name proved that we were back in the region of watering-place walks, for anything that is called 'Ruh' or 'Blick' is closely connected in my mind with a summer-house-like erection built on some jutting piece of rock and ornamented with the edible leavings of sundry picnicing parties. Not that I suggest for a moment that the inhabitants of Badenweiler do anything so vulgar as picnicing, but the association of ideas was too strong for us, and we fled, leaving the Sophien Ruh under the dark suspicion of being ornamented with the carved names of celebrated (?) visitors and littered with paper and orange peel. With this unexpected, but none the less agreeable, ascent of the Blauen, our stay came to an end and the next morning saw us on our way to Freiburg, which lies a short railway journey from Badenweiler and makes an admirable starting-point for a ramble through the great Hollenthal. But for this reason I doubt if we should have taken Freiburg into our scheme of things, for it is an undeniable *town* and we were already beginning to hunger after the simplicity and quiet of the forests. Hence we put up at an hotel nearest the station, with the intention of keeping our stay down to the limit of a day and a night before starting eastwards again. Nevertheless, in spite of its eighty thousand inhabitants, its handsome opera-house, university, garrison, and other greatnesses, we began to feel the old-world charm creep over us, and our regret at the 'wasted time' vanished.

In truth Freiburg is one of the most beautiful towns in Germany, and rivals Heidelberg in its claim to be the pearl of Baden. Side by side with all its modern convenience it retains in a hundred hidden corners relics from its long and stormy history, and the forest-covered hills which shield it on the east have seen a changing pageant of the world's great ones, and bloody pictures of battle and siege, such as few places can remember. Thus it was on a point of rising ground lying to the south and called to-day the 'Bergle' that in 1644 General Mercy, at the head of the Bavarian troops, made a desperate stand against the French under Condé. The encounter cost both sides heavily, but Freiburg, as always, paid the highest price of all : her suburbs lay in ruins, and her monasteries, which had been unwisely built outside her walls, were razed to the ground. To commemorate these misfortunes the Loretto Chapel was erected, but this act of piety seems to have been of little avail, for exactly a hundred years later the French Marshall de Coigny took up his position on the same spot, having found it an admirable vantage-point for the bombardment of the town. Louis xv. himself watched the work of destruction from the Loretto Chapel, and an iron cannon-ball, which to-day is to be found embedded in the wall above the chapel door, testifies to the fact that the monarch nearly paid for the entertainment with his life. As a punishment for this ungrateful and disrespectful act, Freiburg was reduced to a state of ruin for about the seventh time, and one can but wonder that after all these discouraging experiences she did not give up her existence altogether.

From the beginning her history had been marked by stormy changes. Founded by a Zähringer in 1091, she passed into the hands of the Uracks, who from that time styled themselves the Counts of Freiburg; but the new lords were so little loved that in desperation the town put itself under Austrian protection. It appears to have been a case of 'out of the frying-pan into the fire'; but this state of things lasted about four hundred years, during which time the town suffered not only for other peoples' quarrels, but bore the brunt of the Peasants' War. In 1806 she returned to the family Zähringer, and since then has known a peaceful and uninterrupted development. Still, traces of her warlike past remain. On our way back from the Loretto Chapel, which lies to the south-west of the town, we passed through the picturesque Schwalben Thor, a last remnant of the old defences. On the inner

wall a curious picture, representing a peasant
with a cart, illustrates a popular story which
typified the tendency of the Alemannen to make
fun of their Swabian neighbours. A rich
Swabian peasant, having made up his rather
dull mind to buy Freiburg, came to the town
with two sacks full of gold and casually
inquired—

"Was kostet's Stad'le?" (What does this
bit of town cost?) The amusement of the
Freiburgers reached its climax when a further
investigation proved that the gold-sacks con-
tained in reality nothing but sand, the peasant's
wife having performed the exchange—possibly
in order to prove that the Swabian women,
at least, are as sharp as their neighbouring
sisters.

Leaving the old gate behind us we rambled
out of the town and followed the road which
leads upwards to the Schlossberg. As the
name suggests, two castles once guarded the
rocky eminence, but the wars of 1744 reduced
them to ruins, and now little remains to be
seen but a few broken walls, which have been
mercifully left by the busy vine growers. But
the view is justly famous, and having enjoyed
a midday refreshment at the restaurant, we
wandered to the Ludwigshöhe, from whence the
finest panorama can be obtained. To the left

the high mountains draw together, and through
the afternoon haze we caught a glimpse of the
entrance to the Höllenthal, which was to be
the scene of our future wanderings, and closer
at hand the wide and fruitful Dreisam Valley,
dotted with villages and groups of residential
houses. A convenient plan, set up for the use
of ignorant wanderers, pointed out to us the
distant heights of our old friend, the Blauen,
whose almost purple colouring, intensified by
distance, explained the origin of its name, and
in the Rhine Valley the mysterious Schonberg
caught our attention.   The legend which is
connected with this mountain reminds one of
the Venusberg in *Tannhäuser*, with the difference that the pilgrims returning from Rome
with the budding branches of forgiveness were
compelled to excavate in the mountain itself
before they found the dead body of the knight
on horseback. The beauty who had tempted
him from the paths of virtue remained undiscovered, and it is probable that one of the
curiously formed grottos which are to be found
in the country round about gave rise to the
whole story. At any rate, it is understood that
the most susceptible may visit Schonberg
without danger, and the fine view should
recompense him for the two hours' journey and
non-appearance of Frau Venus, who has either

reformed her ways or found the region too dull and moved her quarters to a country where her charms are better appreciated.

Looking away from this once enchanted mountain, our eyes wandered over the Rhine Valley and rested for a moment on the Wiehre, a suburb of Freiburg, lying on the south side of the river Dreisam. The name 'Wiehre' reminded my German friend that we were in the land of witches, and that the Wiehre in particular had once been so famous for these dangerous old ladies that an executioner of the time won a wager by betting that there were more witches in the village than could be got into a four-horse wagon. In truth the unfortunate folk enjoyed a most unenviable lot, and as the Kandel—a high mountain situated in the north-west between Freiburg and Waldkirch—was popularly supposed to be the abode of evil spirits, both towns were ready to torture any old woman on the slightest evidence—age and a sharp tongue being looked upon as enough to arouse and justify the worst suspicions. Accusations of witchcraft were the order of the day, and spurred on by the clergy and the Austrian government, the people of Freiburg let scarcely a month pass without erecting a bonfire for the benefit of some hapless old dame. In the mountains, where ignorance and the tyranny of the clergy were particularly rampant, it was the custom to lay the effects of a storm at the door of the first unpopular old woman who was too weak to offer any resistance, and to put her to death on the charge of having made bad weather. The last witch to be burnt in this part of the country was an old woman of Endingen on the Kaiser-stuhl, who in 1751 was put to death by order of the Catholic faculty because, through an act of carelessness she had set fire to a house. A few years afterwards the Empress Maria Theresa forbade the practice, which had already been put down in the Protestant regions, and old age was at last safe from popular and religious fanaticism.

It might be mentioned that the Jews in Freiburg fared scarcely better; but in spite of the fact that in the fourteenth century they were totally exterminated, their power nowadays is such that in some branches of trade, and notably in agricultural matters, the peasant suffers severely. Hence, even to-day a Jew in the Black Forest is looked upon with hatred and distrust, and he usually confines his attentions to the actual trading in the towns.

All this information I reaped from my companion, who then pointed to the north-west, to the graceful outline of a mountain which rises in solitary grandeur out of the Rhine Valley. Its solitude reminds one a little of the Hohentwiel, but the whole extended form, with its varying and rounded peaks, is gentler, more pastoral. It is the Kaiserstuhl, so called because in past ages it was dimly supposed to have been the Imperial seat of justice. On the highest point—the Todtenkopf (1677 feet)—there once grew an old lime tree, with nine mighty shoots, under whose shade the great Rudolf of Habsburg held his court of justice. The trees yielded at last to the ravages of the storms, and though nine other lime trees have been planted to take their place they have not the historical interest, nor, as yet, the beauty of their predecessors. Strictly speaking, the Kaiserstuhl does not belong to the Black Forest, the very nature of its vegetation, which includes scarcely any pine wood, makes it essentially a contrast; but the traveller who has gone as far as Freiburg would do well to extend his journey to this interesting region. The vineyards which grow round the foot of the mountain give no idea of the wonderful growth of flowers and rare plants which are to be found on the higher points. Especially in spring the Kaiserstuhl resembles a veritable fairy garden, decked with lilies-of-the-valley, anemones, orchids, and covered with the rich purple of the Pulsatilla. The traveller who has a day to spare cannot do better than take the train from Freiburg to Ihringen and thence walk the whole length of the Kaiserstuhl over the Todten-kopf and the Katherinenberg to Endingen, where the railway is once more at hand to transport him back to Freiburg. The whole walk requires about four hours, and offers an unrivalled view over Alsace, the Vosges, the Black Forest, and, on a clear day, the south horizon reveals the pale shimmer of Mont Blanc. The Katherinen-berg, be it remarked in passing, possesses a chapel dedicated to St. Katherine—which St. Katherine is not clear—and in its present form was erected in 1862. The original, how-ever, was founded by a noble and pious lady in 1388, but having suffered not only from wind and weather, but from the godless hands of the warriors of the Thirty Years' War, it fell into disuse until a certain peasant dis-covered its existence, and being also of a holy frame of mind had it repaired as a hermitage.

But I have wandered far afield—be it con-fessed—to another and earlier rambling period, and from our position on the Ludwig's Hohe in Freiburg there are other things to be seen. Thus at our feet lies the town itself with the graceful,

noble Dom rising, like an inspired thought trans-
formed to stone, out of the midst of the clustering
houses. I know no other cathedral in Germany
and, indeed, in Europe which arouses quite the
same feeling of admiration and reverence as this
Freiburger Dom. The Cologne appears clumsy,
ostentatious compared to the wonderful poetry
which lies hidden in every line of this most
perfect architectural expression of German
character. For, indeed, to me there is something
in the whole building essentially Teutonic: there
is poetry, an almost ethereal, unreal beauty in
the inimitable spire, which from a distance looks
like a piece of the most delicate lace-work cut
in rich red sandstone; there is also a certain
lack of harmony in the outline, a certain ruggedness, therefore, mingled with strength and sweetness which makes one feel that the builder
unconsciously has erected a monument to the
genius—the 'Geist'—of his race. Who the
builder was no one knows, though his portrait
is to be found cut in stone in the first tower
gallery. The work was begun under Konrad of
Zähringen in the beginning of the twelfth
century. By 1146 the building was so far
advanced that the holy Bernard of Clairvaux
was able to preach the Crusades from its pulpit.
Nevertheless the cathedral was not actually
finished until nearly a hundred years later, and

small additions were made as late as the sixteenth and seventeenth centuries, hence a certain lack of uniformity in style and construction. In spite of this failing — if failing it be — the cathedral represents a definite idea logically carried out. The extreme simplicity of the body of the building is a deliberate preparation for the increasing richness of design, finding its culmination in the spire, which, though often imitated, has no rival in the world. A minute description of the architectural beauties of the Dom would take me too far from our rambles, and there are guides and guide-books enough—more than enough—to tell the inquirer everything he could want to know; but he who has been to Freiburg and not viewed the cathedral from the Ludwig's Höhe, not wandered about before the wonderful western façade, not lingered in the dim light of the majestic aisle, nor climbed his way up to the belfry, with its thirteen mighty bells, and higher still to the topmost platform of the spire, from whence the whole beauty of the cathedral lies revealed, has missed one of the greatest wonders which Germany has to show.

Close to the cathedral stands the Kaufhaus, a one-storeyed building also in red sandstone, and an interesting example of the transition from

FREIBURG CATHEDRAL.

Gothic to the Renaissance period. But of this there is little to be seen from our elevated position : the spire seems to reduce its surroundings to a humble uniformity, and we turn our eyes northwards towards the Zahringen Burg, which lies at about two and a half hours' walk from Freiburg over the suburb Herdeon and past the well-known Gasthaus zum Jagerhäuschen. Though little remains of the ruins it is of interest as one of the oldest castles on the upper Rhine and the residence of the first of the Zähringen race. The legend has it that a poor peasant having discovered a silver mine in the mountain amassed great wealth, with which he helped a deposed emperor, who had taken refuge on the Kaiserstuhl, back to his throne. As a reward the peasant was made Duke of Zähringen and—of course—married the emperor's daughter. He built the town of Freiburg in Switzerland and also the village and castle of Zähringen; but apparently his new greatness acted deleteriously on his character, for he became notorious as a tyrant and evil-doer, and not even the monasteries of St. Peter and St. Trudpert, which he built in a fit of remorse, could save him from the punishment dealt out to such persons by all respectable legends. After death he was banished, in the form of a stone figure— the prince with the heart of stone—to a distant mountain by the sea, and to this day he is supposed to be paying the penalty of his sins. The legend refers probably to Berthold v., whose stone statue is to be found in the cathedral and of whom history has nothing but evil to relate. With the extinction of the Zahringen house— the present grand‑ducal family belongs to another line—the castle passed into the hands of the Counts of Freiburg, and in the course of the bloody quarrels between the latter and their subjects the castle was reduced to ruins. After having been built up again, and passing from one owner to another, it was finally destroyed in the Thirty Years' War. So much for the surroundings as the Ludwig's Hohe revealed them to us! There are as many more places that I have not mentioned which could keep the traveller occupied for days in rambling about Freiburg, but the Spirit of the Black Forest beckoned us from the rocky entrance to the Hollenthal, reminding us that we were but on the outskirts of her territory and that she had much more to show us. At the same time, in case the reader should ever come to Freiburg and have more time at his disposal, I cannot refrain from recommending two other rambles, the one to the pilgrimage chapel of St. Ottilien, the other to the Hexenthal (Witches' Valley). The former spot is reached by the road which leads past the Kanonenplatz and the ruins of an old Carthusian monastery (1346) at the east side of the town, through beautiful pine forest up to the Roszkopf. After an hour's walking the traveller meets the first of the stations that warn him that he is near the place of pilgrimage itself. Legend traces the founding of the chapel, which lies in the thick of the forest, back to the year 680, when Ottilie, the daughter of an Alsatian duke, fled from her father for some unknown but certainly righteous reason, and in the hour of her need was saved from his wrath by the rocks, which opened and swallowed her up. Overcome by remorse the duke built a chapel on the holy spot, and the waters which from that hour sprang from the rock became celebrated for their power of curing all diseases of the eye. Judging from the many offerings which ornament the chapel, their mysterious and healing influence has been left them ; but in any case a pilgrimage to the chapel is not wasted, and the pilgrim is free to choose any of the beautiful forest paths which lead back to Freiburg.

The Hexenthal is best traversed with a carriage, but a good walker should be able to reach Bollschweil in all ease and comfort in about two hours, and should his energies then forsake him he can either continue as far as

Staufen, where the railway is at his disposal, or make use of the automobile service between Freiburg and Bollschweil. The name of the valley is to be traced back to the story of an old peasant woman, 'Annele,' who refused to join in with the general lamentations over the effects of a disastrous storm, but went about shaking her head and mumbling, 'Selber tun, selber haben,' or, roughly translated, 'Work yourself, get yourself.' This peculiar behaviour gave rise to the suspicion that she knew more about the storm than a human person should know—that, in fact, she had been the wilful cause of the whole trouble; but the judge, do what he would, could not drag a confession out of her. At last, in a fit of temper, he declared that she was a stupid old woman and no witch, which so hurt her dignity that she promptly turned her apron into a rabbit with long ears, which, on investigation, disappeared. Poor Annele had to pay dearly for this piece of bravado. She was immediately bound to a stake and burnt on the spot, which to-day is called the 'Hexenmättle.' As a matter of fact a little old woman with a straw hat, a fur coat, and one white and one red stocking still haunts the valley—perhaps the spirit of the boastful Annele searching for her lost rabbit. Personally, I have not met her, but then our visit to the

BADENWEILER AND FREIBURG

Hexenthal was of the briefest—a mere after-noon's drive through the Bollschweil—and the next day the train bore us away from Freiburg, the land of witches, to another and wilder region, the Höllenthal.

CHAPTER X

THROUGH THE HÖLLENTHAL TO GUTACH

HITHERTO I have endeavoured as much as possible to translate the names of the various places we have visited in order that their full significance—and many of them have a significance—may be apparent to the reader not acquainted with the German language. But the Hollenthal makes me hesitate. What would paterfamilias, on a tour through the Black Forest, say to the idea of conducting his offspring through the Valley of Hell? Well, the word is out now, and if any one is shocked I can only protest that I am not responsible for the outspokenness of the wicked German, and that the Hollenthal is in reality a very beautiful and entirely respectable region. Still, it must be admitted that the originators of the name must have had something infernal in their minds, for at the entrance to the valley we find ourselves at the station 'Himmelreich' (Kingdom of

Heaven), which suggests that a traveller on leaving the Höllenthal behind him, and seeing for the first time the wide, fruitful valley of the Dreisam, with the Dom spire in the distance, feels himself, by comparison, in another and a better world. Still, bold ramblers as we were, we allowed our luggage to proceed on its way per train, whilst we braved the dangers of the region on foot.

The journey through the Hollenthal is one of those where great discretion must be used in the method of procedure. The rambler who insists on doing the whole distance from Freiburg on foot loses time and energy to no purpose, the luxurious one who can afford a carriage indulges in an unnecessary expense, and the most foolish of all, he who clings to the railway in the hope that he will be able to see enough from the window, loses the finest part of the scenery. The wise travellers (ourselves, for instance) make use of the train as far as Himmelreich, and then spread the four hours' walk over the rest of the day, making halts and side excursions where their fancy pleases. As a matter of fact, the grandest part of the scenery confines itself to a comparatively short stretch between the Hirschsprung and the Ravenna - Schlucht, and the rest of the way can be safely traversed with the railway without fear of missing anything of importance.

The railway itself, as so often in the Black Forest, is one of the 'sights,' and it amused us as we tramped along the well-kept road to watch some black puffing monster wending its way along the side of the precipice, disappearing in yawning tunnels, only to appear again some distance ahead with a shriek of triumph. As a matter of fact the railway, wonderful as it is, remains a failure, except from a tourist point of view. Various errors of judgment, such as the constant repetition of unnecessarily sharp curves, have considerably reduced the speed, and the necessary use of the cog-wheel system from Hinterzaiten has made the transport of heavy goods an impossibility. Compared to the Black Forest railway proper, the Hollenthal Bahn has nothing wonderful to show, but it is undeniably useful, and we, at any rate, were sincerely grateful to the State for having performed a useful task.

As for the road, along which we wended our way, its first origin is unknown. It appears that it was laid in order that the Princess Marie Antoinette might be brought to France as much as possible over Austrian territory, but it is also certain that a good road of some sort must have existed beforehand, though possibly not always leading over the same ground. As it stands

174

to-day it is one of the finest in the Black Forest, and as we tramped up the increasingly steep gradations we pictured the wonders of a bicycle tour from the highest point down to Freiburg and for the first time wished that we had started at the other end.

In any case, whether he starts from Freiburg or from Titisee, the rambler with his bicycle may count on a pleasant ride, only, if he go from Freiburg, he must be prepared to 'foot it' occasionally, and if from Titisee he must be strong of nerve and not allow the joys of free-wheeling to run away with his discretion. But 'revenons à nos moutons' and to our wholly dangerless wanderings from Himmelreich to the first grandeurs of the Höllenthal! Shortly after we had left the little station behind us, my companion, who never lets anything escape her alert eye, discovered the ruins of Burg Neu-Falkenstein towering above us from the summit of the rocks which were beginning to close in on either side. The Neu-Falkenstein Burg was, she informed me, only a kind of branch establishment of the actual Burg Falkenstein which we were to pass farther along the road. Legend surrounds both castles with a halo of romance, and the name 'Falkenstein'—according to the legend—is to be traced back to a remarkable episode. A certain Konrad von Stein, one of

the first owners of the castle, was deeply troubled
by the fact that his marriage remained childless,
and having been instructed by a dream, started
off on a crusade with Gottfried von Bouillon in
order to propitiate Heaven into granting him his
wish. At parting he divided his wedding-ring
with his wife, and made her promise him to wait
at least seven years for his return. The unfortunate gentleman, however, fell into the
hands of the Saracens, and the seven years
passed before he succeeded in making his escape.
Again a dream—in those believing days it was
always a dream which helped the story-teller
over those nasty hitches in the train of circumstance which worry the modern novelist—warned
him that his wife was on the point of marrying
another, and on awaking the knight made a
compact with the devil, who had been simply
awaiting the occasion. The compact was that
the devil should transport Konrad back to his
castle, but should the latter fall asleep on the
road his soul should become the devil's property.
No sooner agreed than the devil became a lion
which caught up the alarmed crusader and started
with him on the long journey. Time after time
the knight overcame the agonising need of sleep,
and at the critical moment, just when temptation
was getting the better of him, a white falcon
was sent from heaven, and perching itself on

his head, so maltreated him with wings and
beak that he had no choice but to keep awake.
The cheated devil thereupon set him down at
the gates of his castle, already thronged with
the wedding guests, and the dishevelled pilgrim
reached his wife in time to prevent the second
marriage. It is said that the wife at first refused
to recognise her husband, but as he produced
his half of the ring her half immediately flew to
rejoin itself in a complete circle, which even for
the most sceptical was uncontrovertible proof.
At any rate, 'All's well that ends well': the
disappointed bridegroom took to his heels, and
as a token of his gratitude Konrad von Stein
added a white falcon to his coat of arms and
called his castle 'Falkenstein.' But, alas! the
legend, as usual, corresponds but little with the
true facts of the case. Truthful history relates
that the Falkensteiners were robber knights of
the worst character; their wives even took part
in the work of catching and plundering the un-
fortunates who were signalled from the outposts
at Neu-Falkenstein, and for this and their general
cruelty they were hated by neighbours and
peasants alike. But one day a woman, whose
husband and newborn babe had been brutally
murdered, and who herself had barely escaped
with her life, succeeded in raising the Freiburgers
to action. With the help of the neighbouring

knights the Castle Falkenstein was taken by storm in the middle of the winter 1390 and razed to the ground. The common folk were put to death, but the real culprits, the lords of the castle, were allowed to go free after having sworn a great oath of allegiance to their conquerors. Whether they kept it or not history does not relate, but their castle was never rebuilt, and the present-day neighbours are firm in their assertion that the place is haunted with the spirits of the Falkensteiner victims whose bones lie buried amongst the ruins.

From the Neu-Falkenstein onwards our road led us through a region of increasing wildness; the rocky walls of the valley drew in closer around us and rose up like rugged towers, crowned at the summit with grand weather-beaten pines. At one point, where the valley becomes scarcely more than a narrow gorge, we looked up to the Hirschsprung, a mighty precipice, which seems to overshadow the pass beneath like some watching giant, and beheld the silhouette of what appeared to be a stag, preparing to leap over the chasm to the opposite side. The stag, unfortunately, turned out to be a bronze figure, whose tasteless existence at the finest part of the ravine is supposed to commemorate a legendary feat performed by some hunted stag in bygone days. We had already seen another 'Hirschsprung' in the Wehra Valley, and I might mention that wherever a precipice is faced within reasonable distance by another precipice, the place is sure to be called the Hirschsprung, and the natives will all be equally ready to perjure themselves with some unlikely account of the origin of the name. Altogether the repetition of names in the Black Forest is most misleading; there are, for instance, two or three valleys bearing the name of 'Gutach,' and it behoves the traveller to be careful or he will find himself in the east when his desired destination lies due west. Be it made clear, therefore, that our road through the Hollenthal was to bring us to the Gutach that lies north of Donaueschingen on the banks of the river Gutach.

From the moment that we left the Hirschsprung behind us the valley lost something of its interest; the rocks on either hand drew back, and the fresh green which covered the mountainsides, though a change after the barren ravine by the Hirschsprung, reduced the valley to the level of many others which we had seen. Thus we were not altogether sorry when another hour's walk brought us to Hollsteig, where we had promised ourselves dinner at the Gasthaus zum Stern, a pleasant little inn lying deep down in the valley at the foot of the Kaiserwachtfelsen. The advice of our host, who watched over us with a fatherly interest as we hungrily attacked our trout dinner, led us to change our original plan of walking the rest of the way to Titisee through the Hollenthal. He pointed out to us that we had already seen the most beautiful part of the Hollenthal, and that it was worse than criminal to leave Höllsteig without paying a visit to the Ravennaschlucht, which was *the* pearl of the Black Forest. We had by this time encountered a good many 'pearls,' but our host was so decided about the matter, and seemed to look upon the gorge so much in the light of a personal possession, that we felt that there was nothing for it but to give way. Thus, after a brief survey of the surroundings, which had once more assumed the wild and rocky character of the lower valley, we wended our way down the path to the great viaduct, the finest piece of engineering which the whole Hollenthal railway has to show. Measuring over four hundred feet in length it is supported by three mighty stone pillars and leads over the Ravennaschlucht to the last stiff ascent to Hinterzarten. But our way lay beneath the viaduct, along a narrow path, and then up roughly cut steps, but always at the side of the foaming Ravennabach (why it is called 'Ravenna' is not certain, but presumably the name is derived from 'Raben,' raven). Twenty minutes' climbing brought us over a fine waterfall to the Ravennafelsen and thence once more on the high-road. Had the time allowed, we might have continued to follow the gorge as far as the Schanz, from whence a fine view can be obtained over the upper Hollenthal, but in the first place we were anxious to catch the train from Hinterzarten to Titisce, and in the second we had been warned that the path was sorely neglected and almost impracticable. Even as it was we found the gorge quite sufficiently troublesome to negotiate, and we were glad enough to accept the services of the puffing and snorting little train which at Hinterzarten discards the cog-wheel for the ordinary rails. For we were now in the Black Forest Highlands, a new region as wonderful as, if entirely different from, the wilderness of rock and forest that the Hollenthal had revealed to us. As we watched the straggling village of Hinterzarten disappear into the background we felt that by some miracle we had climbed up into a high plain, into a broad pastoral valley yet swept with pine-laden mountain winds and roofed by a sky which somehow seemed to have come closer to us. We had, indeed, a feeling that we had been brought nearer to heaven than we had ever been before—a very correct state of mind after our pilgrimage through the

Höllenthal—and we were grateful for the inspiration which had led us to take up our night quarters at Titisee, which lies in the very heart of the Highlands. But it is a mistake to be grateful for inspirations until one sees where they take one. Somehow or other a cold chill of disappointment settled on our spirits as we descended from the railway carriage and gathered together as many of our possessions as we required for our short stay. I think we scented already from afar off the familiar atmosphere of St. Blasien's cheap smartness and our old acquaintances the sociable would-be society folk. We were not, unfortunately, mistaken in our apprehensions. The table d'hôte at the Schwarzwald Hotel (situated on the borders of the lake and fairly comfortable when not overcrowded) revealed their actuality to a depressing degree, and we consumed our dinner in sulky silence, surrounded on all sides by smart would-be sporting young men, and smart would-be fascinating maidens trying to charm the masculine element by high spirits and alluring sweetness. They belonged essentially to the class which patronises cheap Swiss Alpine resorts and jumps up every five minutes from the dinner-table to rush to the window and gape at a real or imaginary 'Alpine glow'; if the reader has ever sunk so low—paradoxically—as to visit a cheap

Alpine resort he will understand what I mean and sympathise. Half deafened by the general chattering—shouting would scarcely be a too strong expression—we hurried away out of the hotel grounds and tried to lose ourselves, or rather our fellow-creatures, in a long evening ramble about the borders of the lake. Fortunately our fellow-creatures on this occasion were not of the type that likes going far afield from its own species, and ten minutes' quick walking put us out of hearing of the giggling crowd and left us in undisturbed enjoyment of the twilight and the lake. In the light of the fading evening the popular Titisee did not disappoint us : there was a peaceful charm about its quiet, unruffled waters which acted soothingly on our tired and decidedly ruffled spirits ; the low mountains, rising gently from the banks, expressed peace if not grandeur, and there was a gentle melancholy in the silence that was not untouched with the mystery which belongs to the Spirit of the Black Forest—when she is undisturbed.

"What a lovely place the world would be without the people in it!" my German friend murmured, still sore with her table d'hôte experiences and apparently labouring under the delusion that some extraordinary superiority separated her from the rest of the despised human race. I sympathised too deeply to dis-

183

illusion her, and together we lingered in the dusk, waiting to hear the ringing of the church bells which lie deep below the surface of the waters. For whereas there are some that say the name Titi comes from 'Tinten,' ink, there are other and wiser folk who maintain that the word is derived from 'titimire,' to ring, and tell a sad story of a town and a monastery which were swallowed up by the waters as a punishment for a wanton luxury. Later the waters of the lake threatened to burst into the Hollenthal and sweep away the whole of the Dreisam Valley, but an old witch stopped up the opening with her night-cap and averted the catastrophe, proving, therefore, that even witches have their uses and should be propitiated. Unfortunately a thread of the night-cap wears out every year, so that unless some other friendly old soul is persuaded into sacrificing her head-gear the danger will become imminent, and I advise the rambler to make haste if he wishes to visit the Titisee in safety. For the rest the Titisee is about half an hour's walk in length, a quarter of an hour across, and about one hundred and twenty feet deep. This latter fact should only be mentioned in a whisper, as it is a fearful and dangerous subject. One of the few who attempted to plumb the dark depths was warned by a terrible voice that if he continued his impertinent investigations he would

THE TITISEE.

be swallowed up, and since then no one has inquired further into the matter. Probably it was a man from Cook's who eventually risked his life to satisfy Anglo-Saxon curiosity—the natives would never have been so disrespectful to their own legends.

Stripped of its legend and an all-beautifying sunset the Titisee can scarcely be reckoned to be one of the most beautiful Black Forest lakes. It is too bald and, in spite of its height (2574 feet), too hot in the midday sunshine to make it a pleasant resort at any other than in the early season. That it is always overcrowded proves less than nothing, and the traveller who has been tempted so far would do well to follow in our footsteps as we walked early the next morning through the opening of the Bärenthal to Erlenbruch.

We were now once more in the region of the Feldberg, having travelled from the south-eastern corner of the Black Forest to the western corner and once more east, and our road brought us to the banks of the Seebach, which we had met once before under the names of Gutach and Wutach. In fact, peaceful Boll seemed almost within calling distance, though many miles of sometimes arduous and sometimes luxurious journeying separated us from our starting-point.

From the village of Bruderhalde we looked up to the broad back of the Feldberg, which divided us from Todtnau, and then the valley narrowed and took on something of the wild, rugged character of the Feldsee, the Gutach's birthplace. We could easily imagine that this wilderness had once well merited its name of the Bear's Valley, until in the year 1611 the first bold pioneers attacked their lairs and after much strenuous labour won the valley for themselves. Even to-day the region is solitary enough ; save for the inhabitants of the quiet village we met few wanderers, and the social folk of Titisee seemed to ignore the place altogether. I hope I shall not seem unduly misanthropic if I confess that the fact caused me no severe heartburnings. Yet we cannot exactly lay claim to having discovered the Bärenthal and its charms. Three quarters of an hour's walk brought us to Erlenbruck, where a pleasant little Gasthaus (zum Schwan) showed us that there were other ramblers who preferred· simple fare and peaceful idyllic surroundings to the noisy pretentiousness of popular resorts. Here for 5 marks a day the visitor may enjoy all that the Black Forest has to show in the beauty of wood and moor, rock and sunlit pastures, and his must be an exacting constitution which does not take in fresh strength with the pure mountain air as it comes down from the Feldberg heights. Naturally the rambler must not expect too much for his 5 marks a day, but as in Boll, so here, every reasonable comfort is at hand, and many of the discomforts of hotel life are absent. Had we not bound ourselves to a certain afternoon train which was to take us away from Titisee's unloved inhabitants, we might have relapsed from our energetic wanderings into a week's *dolce far niente*. But destiny, in the form of our departed luggage, called us to other and, as we were to experience, less peaceful adventures. The railway journey from Titisee to Donaueschingen took us through the changing scenery which characterises the Black Forest Highlands. Here wide stretches of open country remind us of the Swiss mountain pastures, then suddenly deep wooded clefts such as can be found in the Black Forest only. The large windows which a considerate State had provided for the benefit of travellers on the Black Forest railway allowed us to see and admire from every side, and the time passed in observation and plan-making. Hitherto we had been rather proud of the fact that, flaunting the warnings and advice of all the guide-books that were ever written, we had avoided 'plans' of any sort, and in all our wanderings had never bound ourselves by previous engagement to any particular hotel for any particular period. As the reader has seen, this plan of making no plans had worked admirably. We had never had any real difficulty in obtaining rooms, and where the place had not pleased us we had been free to shake the dust off our feet without any unpleasant discussion with disappointed *hôteliers*. Now for some reason we began to suffer from hitherto unknown misgivings. Our destination, Gutach, had been described to us as a charming village, interesting from the point of view of its people, and known only to artists and the genuine Black Forest lovers, but wholly without hotel accommodation. True, there were three or four Gasthäuser, and we comforted ourselves with their homely names and the assurance that there was bound to be room for us 'somewhere.' Possibly we had become a little 'puffed up' with the success of our haphazard methods, for after a moment's qualms we subsided into the peaceful conclusion that nothing of an unpleasant nature having happened to us so far, nothing unpleasant could happen in the future. Thus the gods blind those whom they are about to destroy. Neustadt and the little town of Höffingen had meanwhile been left behind us : the first named is of comparatively recent origin and has little of interest to offer the visitor ; the second, though its history dates back to distant ages when a savage people offered up their sacrifices on low, undulating hills, can be passed over without serious loss. From certain findings it is known to have been a Roman colony, and in later years the chief meeting-place of the much persecuted Black Forest witches. But these facts did not fascinate sufficiently, and we were content to pass on over our old Boll acquaintance Döggingen to Donaueschingen. Here the necessity of a change of trains gave us an hour in which to make a brief tour of inspection under the guidance of a Donaueschingen friend. With true German courtesy and good-heartedness she had responded to our telegram sent on the 'chance,' and arrived breathless at the station, laden with all the good things which Donaueschingen can supply, and ready to run herself hot and tired in the endeavour to show us as much of her native town as our limited time allowed. And for almost the first time in our rambles we actually 'hustled.' We felt like veritable American tourists as we swept at top speed through the quiet, well-built streets to the so-called source of the great river Danube.

"Of course it isn't really the source," our guide informed us as we stood panting around the marble basin. "As a matter of fact the Danube is formed from the union of the Breg and the Brigach, and this spring, which is drying up, by the way, has really nothing to do with it." Nevertheless, she looked up respectfully at the marble figures of a woman with a young child which decorate the source, and I am sure that at the bottom of her heart she shared the general opinion that they expressed the truth — namely, the figure of the woman represents the country of the Baar pointing to the young source to go forward on its long journey to future greatness, and I felt convinced that it would break the heart of the good Donaueschingen burgher if he really believed that the source was no source at all. He pretends not to believe, just as every self-respecting father pretends not to believe in the unexampled brilliancy and uniqueness of his only son.

Having duly admired the sacred source, which by now has been beautified at the point of its union with the real river by a triumphal monument presented to the Fürst of Fürstenberg by the Kaiser, we were hurried along into further wonders. They were explained to us on the road, and we obtained among other things a vivid account of the disastrous fire which in 1909 burnt practically the whole town to the ground. Fortunately the princely castle was spared, and thanks to the German insurance system no one was much damaged except the insurance companies, and the Donaueschingen of to-day is a modern phœnix of pretty houses and well-built streets. In spite of its small dimensions it is the aristocrat of the surrounding country, and what its inhabitants do not know about court life is not worth knowing. The almost constant residence of the Fürst von Fürstenberg in their midst, and the yearly visits of his close friend the Kaiser, and all the grandeurs which such great ones of the earth bring with them, make the inhabitants feel considerably elevated above ordinary mortals, and we grew quite respectful as our guide talked lightly to us of the recent ball at the castle and her dance with the young prince. In fact, these great ones lay aside their greatness in these secluded regions, and the awe-inspiring Emperor is probably least of all awe-inspiring for his faithful subjects in Donaueschingen, who welcome him regularly when the time comes to shoot the 'Auerhahn.' The Auerhahn (woodcock) is the chief quarry of the Black Forest huntsman, not, I think, for the sake of the flesh, which is tough in the extreme, nor even for the brilliant black plumage, but for the sake of the difficulty which the hunt offers. At ordinary times the Auerhahn's extraordinary fine sight and hearing make it wholly safe from the attacks of man; only in the midst of its own love-song it loses the knowledge of its surroundings, and in the height of its amorous ecstasy the huntsman is at liberty to take up his position in the closest vicinity without fear of being discovered by his prey. Only as the Auerhahn 'balgt,' as it is called, at two o'clock in the morning the hunt still presents sufficient excitement, coloured too with the romance which the hour and the ghost-like surroundings of the forest bring with them.

Donaueschingen lies in the heart of the Auer-hahn's country, and it is well acquainted not only with the Kaiser but with its own particular ruler, the Grand Duke of Baden and his wife. Nor are these modern royalties the only ones whom Don-aueschingen has welcomed. An inscription over the Gasthaus zum Lamm informs—or informed, for I know not if the fire has burnt away the writing—the passer-by that in 1770 the baker Fidelis Schmider was called upon to bake bread for Her Majesty Queen Marie Antoinette of France, whereupon he built the house, probably as a result of his subsequently increased patron-age. So one tragic shadow at least has crossed the threshold of the modest castle—modest, at least when one considers the rank and the wealth of its present owner. For, apart from other matters, the Fürst of Fürstenberg possesses more of the Black Forest than any other land-owner, more even than the Grand Duke himself, and his revenues from that source alone are considerable.

All this information was poured out to us

during a breathless race—it could not be called a ramble—through the park which is Donaueschingen's chief beauty. The wonderful groups of trees, the numerous little lakes and streams, above all the strange varieties of exotic birds, the hundreds of swans sailing in regal dignity on the quiet waters would have held us until evening ; but people who are ' doing' places are bound by time, and before we had half realised what we had seen we were swept back to the station, feeling that we had again left an only half-explored paradise.

"You must come again," our kindly guide gasped as she helped us triumphantly into the train. " I have ever so much more to show you." And then, as the train began to move, she added, " I hope you will be able to find rooms in Gutach. I have hardly ever heard of the place." At this I felt a strange chill of foreboding creep over my spirits, but my German friend retained her unconquerable optimism.

"Don't you see that's the whole charm of the thing," she explained. " Nobody knows of Gutach. We shall have the whole village at our feet." The prospect sounded all that could be desired, and it was with hopeful eyes that we watched the towns of Villingen and St. Georgen slip past us. After all, we had arranged to visit them from Gutach, where we were to take up a lengthier residence in order to enjoy rural simplicity and the simple life! Shortly after St. Georgen we passed the little station of Sommerau and plunged into the first and longest tunnel in the Black Forest railway. Although it does not offer the wonders of one of the Alpine railways, the Schwarzwald Bahn is none the less a fine engineering feat, deserving more financial success than it has obtained. Built in 1873 by the State at a heavy cost, it has never even paid its own working expenses, partly because no heavy goods trains can be used on the line, and only the traveller has gained benefit from the accomplishment of a difficult and expensive task. We felt positively grateful to the benevolent State who—unconsciously, it is true—had prepared such beauties and marvels for us, and it gave us a dizzy pleasure to trace our miraculous curlings in and out, down and round the mountain-side, as we descended slowly but steadily to Triberg. One or two of the corkscrew tunnels reduced us to a state of hopeless bewilderment, changing the whole scenery and bringing us eventually out at some spot hundreds of feet beneath, from whence we could look upwards to the thin, snake-like line which, disappearing suddenly and mysteriously into the face of the rock, marked our starting-point.

From Sommerau to Gutach we descended

1632 feet, and passed through no less than thirty-seven tunnels, measuring together over five miles in length. The reader may complain at the latter feature, but the long incarcerations in the heart of the mountain are well paid for by the wonderful occasional glimpses of wild gorge and distant valley. Thus we passed Triberg and the castle of Hornberg, and our eyes lingered with a certain regret on the fine hotel which looks down on the town beneath from the castle heights. We were tired, the evening gloom, moreover, was increased by the approach of threatening rain-clouds, and the uncertainty of our destination began to lose something of its original charm.

"But of course it will be all right," said my companion, picking out the names of the different Gasthauser from her guide-book with an appearance of unabated cheerfulness. Alas for rural simplicity! The station of Gutach offered all that could be desired in that direction. Its simplicity was almost primitive. No porter, no carriage (of course), no ticket-collector, nobody and nothing save an empty platform! There was no choice—we left our luggage to take care of itself and set off on a pilgrimage to the village, which, for no reason that we could discover, was situated half a mile from the station. And then it began to rain! It was pouring in torrents by the time we reached the first little inn, and since it appeared very primitive indeed we felt that we ought to live up to our professions and ask for lodging. I suppose we did look rather doubtful characters now that I come to think of it. We had no luggage, our clothes were soaked through, our faces bore the traces of the thirty-seven tunnels —it was not surprising that the innkeeper's wife looked upon us with grave suspicion.

" Yes, she had rooms," she admitted, and then we drew a sigh of relief; " but they were taken ten minutes before by two gentlemen."

We took to the road again in gloomy silence. Somehow we neither of us believed in the existence of those two 'gentlemen,' and our feelings were hurt. The village was not showing the interest and respect which we had expected, and our joyful admiration of the verdant valley was tinged with bitterness as we reached the village itself. Still, there were pretty cottages enough, and our spirits revived somewhat as a kindly faced woman nodded us a friendly greeting from the shelter of her doorway. Encouraged by her sympathetic glance—our condition was by this time wholly pitiable—we ventured to ask her if she knew of any place where we could get rooms. She beamed with the hopefulness which people always feel about other peoples' difficulties.

" Ja, ja," she said, " at the Gasthaus zum

Linden—there, round the corner and over the bridge. All the artist people go there." The reference to 'artist people' left us uncertain as to whether we ought to feel flattered or otherwise. There are artists and artists, and somehow we could not but recognise that our appearance was against us. But the 'Linden' enchanted us. Here was a genuine old Black Forest inn, with thatched roof, weather-burnt wood, quaint gablings, and balconies running beneath the eaves—a veritable gem of its class and situated just opposite the picturesque bridge and the village church, for all the world like the scene on a picture postcard.

"At last!" we exclaimed in one breath, and lost no time in hurrying up the narrow wooden staircase which led to the entrance of what we fondly supposed was our place of refuge. An immense burly figure blocked the doorway, and somehow our spirits underwent a third fit of depression as we looked up into the typical peasant's face, clean-shaven, determined, with thin, compressed lips and keen, suspicious eyes. Unaccustomed as we were to the type, we disliked the man on the spot. We told him we wanted rooms. He looked us up and down.

"Gibt's nicht," he said.

"We must have rooms," we repeated, with the determination of despair.

"Go to the Gasthaus zur Sonne," he advised laconically.

We told him we had already tried there, and related the story of the two 'gentlemen.'

For the first time his features relaxed with the flicker of a smile.

"That was a lie, anyhow," he observed, and somehow his manner inferred that he did not blame the 'Sonne' folk for having resorted to this method of getting rid of such questionable customers. "Anyhow, there is no room here," he repeated stonily.

Now, I do not want to boast of aristocratic connections, but my German friend is a woman of title and accustomed to be treated with the respect and consideration which only a title can obtain in the Fatherland, and she literally shook the dust—or rather mud—off her feet.

"A horrid boor," she said, as we wended our way dismally back to the village High Street. "How I despise these plebs—brutes, all of them!" Fortunately our little shoemaker's wife proved an exception. We turned to her in a last hope, and she took us into her best parlour and watched our dripping clothes make rivulets along her clean scrubbed floor without a murmur. More than that, she sent her husband and her children to the right and left, and soon we had obtained our hearts' desire—the whole

village was congregated around us in good-
natured interest, but, alas! not in admiration.
We felt like a pair of strange and far from
beautiful birds that had fallen into a nest of
chattering sparrows, and we had only one wish
—to get away, anywhere, so long as it was from
rustic simplicity.

As the tenth messenger arrived with the
oft-repeated intelligence that Frau So-and-so's
rooms were taken, we gave up in despair. The
windows of the Hornberg Castle Hotel sparkled
like beacons through the growing darkness, and
with a last spurt of energy we attacked the little
post office (already closed, for it was long past
its business hours), and cajoled the good-natured
post-master into telephoning up to Hornberg.
I think our knees positively shook whilst we
awaited the answer, and nothing can express
our relief as we were informed that two rooms
were reserved for us and a good dinner awaited
our consumption. But how were we and our
luggage to be transported all that distance?
Again our friend the shoemaker's wife came to
our assistance.

"The host of the Linden has a carriage," she
told us; but my German friend's pride rose in
arms. Nothing, not even the prospect of
spending the night in the streets, would induce
her to appeal to the kindness of her deadly

enemy.   So we sent the poor, patient little shoemaker's wife instead.

Two hours later a curious one-horse shay of ancient build drew up at the door of the cheerful Hornberg Schloss Hotel, and two dripping, half-frozen, and very bad-tempered travellers slunk through the well-filled lounge into the merciful privacy of their rooms.   Certainly rustic simplicity has its charms, but it must be properly managed, and haphazard arrivals are better restricted to the large centres.   At any rate, he who would make his stay at Gutach would be wise to make inquiries beforehand, unless, of course, he wants to have the whole village at his feet—as we did.

CHAPTER XI

RAMBLES ROUND ABOUT HORNBERG

OUR awakening on the morning following our disordered flight from Gutach rewarded us for all previous discomforts and disappointments. From our windows, which faced direct north, we gazed on the whole broad and beautiful Gutach Valley to Gutach itself, with its long, straggling village, and beyond to the gently rounded mountains, which, with their protecting pine-covered heights, seemed to shut off the peaceful region from the rest of the noisy, fretting world. And as we watched the morning sunlight flood over the green fields, and the sparkling, hurrying river which flows between them to the cottages, half hidden by the forest outskirts, we felt that we were to learn to know the Black Forest Spirit in a new mood—a wholly pastoral and tender mood—and that the country of wild gorges and seething torrents lay far behind us.

As the day advanced and brought us new experience, our conviction that we had done well to make the Hornberg Schloss Hotel our quarters, at any rate for the time being, became more confirmed. In all our ramblings we had rarely found a hotel more beautifully situated or more calculated to meet the requirements of the traveller who, whilst desirous of moderate comfort, flees the haunts of the ordinary tripper. The situation, above all, is admirable. The Hornberg (1200 feet) juts out over the town like a natural fortress guarding the entrance to the Gutach Valley, and at its summit part of the old ruins of the castle have been replaced by the Hotel, which thus enjoys an uninterrupted outlook over the town nestling at its feet, and over the whole country lying to the north and south. It follows, too, that the air is magnificently pure and fresh, and the peace undisturbed, save for the dreadful occasions when the Kur band, composed of twenty yokels armed with as many brass instruments, comes to make the evening hideous with its distortions of the latest popular airs. These occasions are too rare, fortunately, to form an objection, and as a compensation there are the many charming strolls from the hotel, which do not necessitate a descent into the quiet, old-world town beneath. Naturally, our first exploration was to the tower of the castle, which marks the actual summit of the mountain. A most unromantic penny-in-the-slot arrangement procured us an entrance, and from the platform we obtained an uninterrupted view over the surrounding country, but our chief interest centred itself on the history of the old ruin. Built sometime in the twelfth century, it marks one of the chief centres of the Reformation movement in the Black Forest. The whole of the Gutach Valley community is Protestant, and has been so since the days when Duke Ulrich of Württemberg put his whole power and influence into the service of the new faith. If history relates truly, his methods of promoting the conversion of his people were not always of the gentlest, but at least he obtained his end and also lent much-needed protection to the persecuted leaders of the Reformation. Thus in 1548 he allowed Johann Brentius, a hunted preacher of Luther's doctrine, to find refuge in the Castle of Hornberg, which later also served the Princess Juliane of Württemberg as a pleasant residence during twelve years of her exile. In 1704 the castle was destroyed by the Marshall Villars as a kind of parting blow before he was compelled to evacuate by the army of peasants which had come against him, and since then the ruins have served for purely ornamental purposes.

The town itself dates back to the early centuries, but little of its ancient walls remain. There is nothing to tell of battle, siege, and religious persecution : a sleepy peace lies over its one broad street, and the Protestant and Catholic churches—distinguishable as everywhere in the Black Forest by their respective rounded and pointed-shaped steeples—hobnob within calling distance of each other. Over the bridge to the left, and past the Protestant church, we discovered a narrow path which led us along the outskirts of the forest to the most charming of old cottages, shaded on the one side by fruit trees, on the other by the darker green of pine and fir. Prosperous fields separated us from the river, and every here and there busy peasant women with short skirts and gay-coloured handkerchiefs tied over their heads looked up from their work to nod us a pleasant good-day.

" If only we could see more of the people themselves ! " lamented my companion, who by this time had forgotten her grievances against the 'plebs.' " We outsiders see nothing but the hotel-porters and servants. And some of these peasants have such interesting faces. One would like to see something of their lives and ways."

The Providence who is proverbially supposed to look after three classes of people—we need not go into details—seemed to keep a kindly eye on our wanderings and an open ear for our desires. Quite against our intentions and desires we found ourselves, after an hour's walking along the right bank of the river, at the scene of our disaster — Gutach. Sunshine, blue sky, and good temper are wonderful scenery painters. The grey, inhospitable 'nest' of yesterday had become a charming, long-drawn-out village with gay, white-washed cottages, quaint, picturesque mills, and friendly inns—all clustering like a brood of chickens under the shelter of the simple village church, whose spire, rising high above the low-built buildings, forms a landmark for all the country round. We paused a moment to gaze regretfully at the Gasthaus zum Linden! It looked even more attractive than before, and only our sense of injured pride prevented us from making further inquiries as to future accommodation. Perhaps, too, at the bottom of our hearts we were rather anxious to show ourselves to the suspicious host in all the splendour of our 'best clothes'—the humiliation of the previous day still rankled. And then my German friend was seized with an inspiration— from the guide-book, as I afterwards discovered, but let that pass.

"There is a well-known Black Forest painter here," she told me; "and I understand that he keeps 'open studio' for anybody who likes to look in. Why should we not see what there is to be seen?"

RAMBLES IN THE BLACK FOREST

The idea had its attractions, and after sundry inquiries we found ourselves at the gates of a pleasant little house, distinguishable from its neighbours only by its more modern architecture. There we hesitated. It seemed unwarrantable impertinence ; we were total strangers, and the sunny quiet of the place rebuked intrusion, but courage—or presumption, if you will—won the day, and it was fortunate that it did so, for we were greeted with that simple, unaffected kindness which belongs to the Teutonic people, especially of the south, and for an hour we engrossed ourselves in sketch-books and paintings whilst our host talked of the people he knew so well, and listened smilingly to the story of our Gutach experiences.

"The Black Forest folk are very difficult to understand," he said at last. "At the bottom they are immensely good-hearted and kindly, but they are also proud, reserved, and shy of strangers —not without reason. You have no idea what they have to suffer from the rudeness of the trippers, who look upon them as so many animals dressed up for their amusement. But if you get to know them—and the best time is when there are few strangers about—you will find them an interesting and fine race. Our host of the Linden—Herr Lindenwirt, as he is called—is a case in point. If you will come round with me you will learn to know him in a new light." We were only too pleased to accept this new leadership, and found that our leader had spoken the truth, for as he entered the big, low-ceilinged 'Gaststube' the Lindenwirt's face relaxed into a welcoming smile, which broadened as he saw us bringing up the rear. We were formally introduced, and shook hands as if the contretemps of yesterday had never been.

"Ja, ja," he said in answer to our inquiries, "there is a nice little room empty for next Saturday. And there is the opening of the new almshouse, with all sorts of festivities—that will amuse you. Ja, and Herr L——"—pointing to our companion—"is exhibiting his pictures. Thirty pfennig entrance fee for the benefit of the village charities. Many people will come."

A most excellent dinner, served up under the critical eye of Herr Lindenwirt himself, decided us, and we parted, on the understanding that next Saturday was to witness our arrival and participation in the popular festivities.

"The Herr Lindenwirt (Mr. Host of the Linden) is one of the characters of Gutach," our new friend told us as he accompanied us a little on our way back to Hornberg. "A typical Black Forester, he is as cunning as he is honest, as good-natured as he is distrustful, and as autocratic as a king. He keeps his inn simply for the pleasure of the thing and only takes in such guests as satisfy his very particular fancy. Yesterday you came without proper introduction, and no doubt he suspected you of being 'Malweiber' (lady artists), for whom he has no great love; to-day you have been properly introduced, and unless you do anything to offend him he will treat you as an accepted friend of the family. Only you must remember that he is your host—the money part of the transaction means nothing to him, for he is one of the biggest landowners about here —and treat him with the proper respect and courtesy. On his side he will treat you as his personally invited guests."

We promised to do our best to follow his advice, and with a hearty 'Aufwiedersehen' and repeated thanks, we continued on our way alone, well satisfied with the harvest which our daring had reaped for us.

On our return to Hornberg we discovered that our much-missed, often-longed-for bicycles had arrived, having been sent for after we had experienced the virtues of the Black Forest roads At the same time it is only fair to warn the traveller that if he bring his bicycle with him on his Black Forest travels he must be prepared to part with it for long periods, and, indeed, regard it as a *modus operandi* for special occasions only. For, indeed, the most beautiful parts of the country are closed to the cyclist, and only in the valleys, as in Gutach, can he make use of his machine. But he who gives himself the trouble to work out his route carefully, and does not mind entrusting his machine to the tender mercies of railway people, will find it an inestimable boon on the long and beautiful descents from the mountains and through the open valleys, where long distances and unshaded roads make the pedestrian's road a hard and thankless one. Thus we should have been glad to have had our machines through the Alb and Wiese valleys, and in Gutach they proved invaluable, but in other parts of the country they can be more trouble than they are worth.

We began our judicious use of our new possessions by free-wheeling cautiously from our hotel down to the station and once more consigning them into the hands of the railway porter. The beauty of the scenery from St. Georgen down to Triberg had tempted us to retrace our steps, and, moreover, there were the delights of gliding down smooth and winding roads where we had previously been shut up in hot and smoky tunnels. Thus, early on the morning after our second trip to Gutach found us once more at the second highest point of the Black Forest railway, at St. Georgen. The sunny streets and well-built little houses did not suggest a great age or historical past, and yet St. Georgen was one of the first places to know civilisation. Roman pieces of money and the remains of fortifications make it almost certain that a Roman high-road once passed that way, and after the dark interval, when the great Empire had crumbled and no human foot ventured up into the solitudes, St. Georgen was still the first to hear the sound of the axe and the human voice.

Attracted, perhaps, by the seclusion of the place, two noblemen, one a nephew of the Abbot of Reichenau, built the monastery of St. Georgen in the year 1084, and the Pope having taken the building under his special protection, it grew and flourished in spite of more than one serious outbreak of fire. Then came the iron-handed Ulrich of Wurtemberg, whose work in the Gutach Valley we have already mentioned, chased out the Catholic priests, replaced them by Protestants, and compelled the whole country round to accept his faith — which they did, apparently without much ado, since when the pressure was removed they continued in the new ways until this day. But the monastery fell into a ruined state, and nothing remains but an old legend which the Catholic minority tell for the benefit of their Protestant neighbours;

namely, the old monastery possessed a bell called 'Susanna' which refused to ring for the first Protestant service, and on being urged, tumbled out of the steeple and rolled down the hillside. Not to be outdone, the community sent a wagon with ten oxen to bring back the refractory 'Susanna,' who, however, refused to stir in spite of all persuasion. Thereupon one of the oxen drivers lost his temper and blasphemously observed that she would have to hang in the church whether God liked it or not. Immediately oxen, wagon, bell, and drivers continued to roll pell-mell downwards until they sank into an enormous chasm, from which to this very day the believer may hear the ringing of a bell, the groaning of men, and the cracking of angry whips. As I have said, in spite of Susanna's protests, St. Georgen remained Protestant, and accordingly the 'Tracht' affected by the inhabitants is marked by Protestant sobriety. The more gorgeous dress of the women of the Catholic regions is replaced by simple black caps and dark-coloured bodices, with only the white puff sleeves to relieve the general gravity ; but, on the whole, the effect is more pleasing, and the comparative inexpensiveness of the costume, besides its greater utility, has resulted in the Protestant population retaining their 'Tracht' long after the Catholics have sunk to 'modern fashions.' Only the bridal clothes form an exception, and a St. Georgen wedding should never be missed, if only on account of the gorgeous and terrible head-dress which the bride has to carry, with all her other troubles, to the altar. It consists of an immense turban-shaped structure, nearly a foot high, built up out of a gaudy assortment of parti-coloured pearls, glittering stones, and tinsel. Underneath, the long hair is plaited together with red wool, and a magnificent gold-embroidered waist-belt completes the 'wedding' part of the bride's attire. In most cases the crown is handed down from mother to daughter, and in Catholic parts, where a similar edifice is customary, it is usually left in the keeping of the church 'until called for.'

From St. Georgen, whose comparatively up-to-date buildings reminded us that the town is a recent one, having been built out of the ashes of the old village in the year 1865, our road led us up a preliminary hill, from whose summit we obtained a pleasant view over the surrounding country. That which makes St. Georgen an unsuitable spot for a long residence—its extreme openness and lack of shade—is atoned for by the extent of the panorama. For the town is one of the highest in the Black Forest (2424 feet), and its open aspect allows the wanderer an uninterrupted view to the Alps—a view which we were very pleased to admire after the already mentioned hill. But from thence onwards our road sank in agreeable gradations, so that our exertions until we reached Triberg (1600 feet) were of the slightest. Naturally we stopped at Triberg for dinner, for though we had tried to make ourselves independent of guide-books and conventions, generally speaking, we were not strong enough to resist the influence of hundreds and thousands of wanderers who have solemnly declared that Triberg is one of the most beautiful spots in the whole of the Black Forest. And *the* feature of the place is, of course, the waterfall, which, guided by the same influence, we visited as soon as the excellent dinner at the Black Forest Hotel allowed us to enter upon such exertions. But 'exertions' in connection with the Triberger waterfall is a misuse of terms. Nothing could be more easy, for luxuriously minded visitors nothing more delightful, than the ascent at the side of the roaring waters ; at every corner a bench, or a pavilion, or a photographer ready to make you a beautiful picture of yourself and your family with a background which would make the beholder believe that you had been miraculously upheld in the midst of a cataract ; and paths with neatly kept banks, calculated

to make an English gardener envious—what
more could this cultivated, civilised generation
require? The only trouble is the waterfall,
which, in company with this refinement and
order, seems hopelessly out of place. As it
comes tumbling down from a height of over three
thousand feet, cascading over seven magnificent
breaks, it seems to protest furiously against its
compulsory subjection to the gentler tastes of
mankind. We felt as we stood and gazed sadly
at the fourth and finest fall from the portals
of the would-be rustic pavilion that we were
looking upon the broken-hearted performance of
some one-time free and noble forest-spirit which
mankind had captured and tamed for his amusement. And then, in the midst of our reflections,
strange and wondrous sounds fell on our ear
—uncouth gruntings mingled with melancholy
wails and squeaks. We looked at each other,
and then the awful truth dawned on us. It was
the Kur band again, and we turned and fled.
O civilisation, what crimes are committed in
thy name! In truth the Triberger or Fallbach
waterfall, as it is sometimes called, is ruined by
the tasteless attentions of people who believe in
trimming and adorning Nature until she is what
they consider pretty and 'effective.' Thus,
what is in reality the finest fall in the Black
Forest, perhaps even in Germany, is reduced to

an object of sad regret. At night-time lime-
light is thrown on her waters, on specific
evenings she is illuminated with 'red fire' and
fireworks, and the roar of her waters is daily
intermingled with the efforts of the brass band.
It was all very sad to consider—all the sadder
because Triberg is one of the few places in the
Black Forest frequented by English people, and
because, as the hotel-keeper told us, these
atrocities are performed to suit English taste.
Be this as it may, the mellifluous tones of the
band and the prospect of 'Grand Illuminations'
failed to fascinate us, and it was with the sense
of uncharitable relief that we left our fellow-
creatures behind us and reached the solitudes—
comparative solitudes, at least—at the top of the
fall. Here a wonderful outlook over sunny moor
and forest comforted our injured feelings; a
fresh, invigorating wind helped to blow away a
last irritation, and we felt that we were once more
in touch with the untamed, unspoilt Spirit of
the Forest. A comfortable, quiet-looking hotel,
not two minutes' walk from the first fall, was
jotted down in our memory as a place for future
and lengthier sojourns; and then, with a last
glance at the idyllic world about us, we began
the descent into the valley by the high-road. One
of the most beautiful walks this, through forest
and between moss-grown rocks, with sudden,

almost magic glimpses of Triberg lying beneath in the valley. For the first time we realised the significance of the name 'Triberg' (three mountains), for from our superior standpoint we could see how the white little town nestled at the feet of three closely united mountains—the Kroneck, the Kapellen, and the Wallfahrt. The last is so named from the much-visited Wall-fahrtskapelle (Pilgrimage Chapel), whose quaint-shaped tower we could just see above the hillside. We had already had our attention drawn to the chapel's existence by the 'stations' which have been placed along a path over a bridge to the right bank of the waterfall. The origin of the place is a curious and unusual one. At the end of the seventeenth century a regiment of Austrian soldiers were stationed in the neighbourhood, and in the sighing of the wind through the trees the superstitious warriors believed they heard a wondrous and angelic song of praise. On investigation they discovered a picture of the Holy Virgin nailed to a tree—the work of some grateful soul—and came to the natural conclusion that the voices had been paying homage to the holy figure. Being peculiarly pious-minded, the deeply moved soldiers erected a tin covering for the picture out of their meagre pay, together with a collection-box, which bore the inscription, 'Maria patrona militium, ora pro nobis'; and the future offerings made by pilgrims from far and near made it possible for the captain of the regiment to lay the foundation stone to the present chapel. The pilgrimage is still popular amongst the Black Forest folk, but an attempt to make it a seat for a Jesuit order was frustrated by the Furst of Schwarzenberg, who, in 1805, abruptly ordered the newly arrived religious pioneers out of the country.

A short walk brought us back into Triberg itself, and once more mounted on our iron steeds we free-wheeled down the hill, past the station, and out into the high-road which leads to Hornberg. Beautifully situated as it is, Triberg did not recommend itself to us as suitable for more than a day's visit. Its very beauty is not a little the result of its closed-in situation, and the town itself, with its shops, inns, confectioners, and hotels, bears a too modern stamp for the taste of those who wish to learn to know the real Black Forest. I fear I shall be accused of a leaning to abuse all 'popular' places, and all places where luxuriant and spoilt travellers might hope to find their requirements. But I know that, with perhaps one or two exceptions, such travellers will always be discontented with Black Forest hotels; and the man with simple tastes, who comes for pure love of the country, will find places like Triberg overcrowded and spoilt by an attempt at gaiety and smartness. In a word, they are neither fish, flesh, fowl, nor good red herring, and disappoint every one save the incorrigible tripper. So we had no regrets when, after an enjoyable ride down the scarcely perceptible decline, our road brought us once more to peaceful, old-world Hornberg. The ride, or walk, or drive—as suits the inclination—from Triberg to Hornberg is not to be missed, and cannot be made up for by a journey with the railway, which at this point disappears into the face of the mountain. Pastoral meadows alternate with high cliffs and rocky gorges, and at one point where the road leads through a cutting in the face of the mountain the wanderer may look eastwards to the ruins of the old castle of Hornberg. (The castle over the town received its name later.) The few disconnected walls which remain lie between two jutting points of rock, and legend attributes their downfall to the wicked doings of the owners and inhabitants. It is said that one Christmas Eve the riotous and ungodly crew of noblemen and their womenfolk behaved in such an unseemly manner that a stroke of lightning was sent from heaven which destroyed them and the scene of their evil living at one blow. A pious servant who had ventured to warn her wicked masters was rewarded for her charity by being compelled to wander weeping and wailing about the ruins until a kindly youth released her by the three prescribed kisses, though what happened to her afterwards, history, or rather legend, does not relate. With this point of interest the Gutach Valley opens out into the broad and pastoral country which we have already seen from the heights of the Hornberg; the mountains recede on either hand, and the wanderer finds himself, as we did on the following Sunday, in one of the most beautiful as well as the most typical homes of the Black Forest people.

CHAPTER XII

A VILLAGE FÊTE IN GUTACH: PEOPLE AND CUSTOMS

VERY different from our first was our second or rather our third arrival in Gutach; no longer as doubtful strangers, but as known and respected guests, we made a triumphal entry and dismounted at the Gasthaus zum Linden with the assurance which our new position gave us. Very different, too, was our reception at the hands of the Herr Lindenwirt and his pleasant little wife! Though he retained something of his unbending reserve, there was a decided friendliness in his manner and in the half-unwilling smile which crossed his broad, clean-shaven face as he discussed the programme of the next day's festivities.

"Jawohl, there will be fine doings to-morrow if the weather holds," he said, rather as though the 'fine doings' did not altogether meet with his approval. "You will have to be up betimes."

220

COMING BACK FROM CHURCH.

A VILLAGE FÊTE IN GUTACH

I think the remark was intended as a fatherly
hint that we should retire early, for we had
bicycled down from Hornberg in the late evening,
and already a half darkness had crept over the
valley; but there was such a spirit of unrest in
the little village that it affected even us outsiders, and whilst our host was engaged elsewhere we slipped down the wooden staircase,
out of the house, over the bridge, and into
the chief street. It was a wonderful summer's
evening, cool and yet mild, with a clear sky
which changed from blue to emerald, and from
emerald to the softest lilac, deepening at the
horizon to the purple of the mountains, so that
sky and mountains seemed but a continuation of
each other. In spite of the little stream of
laughing and bustling visitors in whose company
we walked, there was an inexpressible peace
over all; the laughter and movement accorded
so harmoniously with the surroundings that it
seemed no more than the distant murmur of the
river and the chatter of birds, and little as we
cared for crowds, we felt that to be amongst
these sturdy-looking people was to come in
contact with a race which from generations un-
counted had listened to the Spirit of the Black
Forest and unconsciously learnt to understand
her meaning. For, whether they know it or not,
these villagers were part and parcel of the valley

221

and of the low-lying mountains on whose wooded sides so many of them have their lonely homesteads. They seemed the human expression of Nature as they had known her from childhood —hardy, weather-beaten, but with fine, regular features and a touch of the picturesque in dress and manner which did not exclude a conscious dignity. We saw more of this dignity on the following morning by the 'Kirchgang' (church parade), which interesting spectacle we should have missed altogether if we had not been aroused from our slumbers by the sound of children's voices beneath our window. We looked out sleepily, and, lo and behold! the little square which divides the Gasthaus from the village church was crowded with the youth of Gutach all dressed in their best 'Tracht,' from the smallest baby upwards, and carrying flower-decked staffs and pretty home-made wreaths. The sight of so much life and colour effectually aroused us, and by dint of much scrambling we managed to creep into the visitors' pew beneath the pulpit before the bell had ceased to toll. For English eyes the interior of the simple white-washed church presented a curious sight. On the left-hand side of the aisle were the womenfolk, almost without exception in their 'Tracht,' solemn - faced and immovable. To my taste the Gutach dress, both for men and

women, is one of the prettiest that the Black
Forest has to show. The women wear a big,
broad-brimmed straw hat covered with red or
black velvet pompons (red or black, according to
the married or unmarried state of the wearer), a
richly embroidered bodice, white sleeves, short,
very full pleated skirts, which allow for a full
display of unusually small and well-made feet
and ankles, encased in black shoes and bright
blue stockings. The hair, which, as with the
majority of German women, is extraordinarily
thick and long, is plaited and tied with broad
ribbon, and a pretty silk apron completes the
Sunday toilet; but not to be forgotten is the
charm of the faces which gaze out solemnly at
you from beneath the gaily decorated head-dress.
As we looked from one to another of the women
who sat to our left—I fear the sermon was
rather lost on us that day—we could not but be
struck by the high percentage of pretty faces.
Nor was theirs a rough type of beauty. Without being aristocratic the features were finely
cut and regular, the eyes large and lovely in
colour, the complexions such as a lady of fashion
might well envy. Even their figures, usually a
weak point, were neat and trim, and their
manners exquisite. Accustomed to English
village folk we expected to be stared out of
countenance, but they seemed not to notice that

there were strangers in their midst, and we felt as though we were sitting opposite so many rows of daintily dressed dolls, so upright, motionless, and expressionless did they remain throughout the service.

The men sat to the right of the aisle—for the most part men belonging to an older generation, grey-haired, with lined, clean-shaven faces and deep-set eyes and somewhat thin, hard-looking mouths. More than the women they bore the peculiar stamp and characteristics of their race. There was nothing exactly haughty or arrogant in their expression, and yet their dignity was conscious—one felt that, even in church, they were holding themselves apart, shutting themselves off from all contact by an iron wall of pride and reserve. They looked, indeed, what they were, men of position in their own world, which for them is the only world—men, moreover, whose position had belonged to their forefathers through long generations. No parvenus these, no men of newly acquired wealth and importance, but aristocrats who would not have felt honoured if the Emperor had offered them the highest title in the land. And their dress was expressive of their mind and attitude. Their long, black velvet coats lined with red, their red waistcoats, long black trousers, made up a costume at once rich and simple. There was

nothing showy or tawdry about them or their
womenfolk, but one felt that these peasants
were people to be considered and respected, and
that they considered and respected themselves.
Although, as in every little district in Germany,
Gutach has its own peculiar dialect, the sermon
was delivered in 'Hochdeutsch' by a young
clergyman, who in England would have been
considered far too good for a small country
place. But German people are everywhere very
critical and particular as regards their clergy :
the stammering curate with his borrowed sermons
is unknown in their churches, since no 'Pfarrer'
is allowed to read his addresses, and a man who
cannot speak fluently and well finds no place.
And the Black Forester is no exception; he
wants sense connected with a personality, so
that even in the most remote villages the
visitor may hope to hear a sermon as good as,
if not better than many which some unfortunate
English congregations of importance are compelled to listen to.

The whole service lasted an hour, and then,
amidst the droning of the organ, we allowed
ourselves to be borne out with the crowd on
to the little church square. Here a pause was
made ; the set faces relaxed into pleasant smiles
of greeting ; there was a general shaking of
hands and a low, intermittent chorus of 'Grüss

Gott!' as peasants from the more distant 'Höfen' (farms) recognised and greeted each other after the week's interlude. But the conversation never rose above a subdued hum, and when presently a stalwart country policeman appeared, sword clanking, in their midst, a profound silence fell on the little group of churchgoers. With severe solemnity the great man then began to declaim the various notices of importance which concerned the village. In the first place, a regiment of Artillery was to be quartered in Gutach in the next few days, and it behoved each villager to get his house in order for the reception of the 'Herren Offizieren' and the soldiers, amongst whom, judging from the beaming face of an old woman beside me, there was at least one Gutach Bauer. Then there was to be a sale of wood by auction, and other matters which this village newspaper thundered out to his respectful listeners with the mien of a man who feels acutely the greatness and responsibility of his task. This over, the crowd of gaily dressed folk began to disperse, and we were left standing in the empty square feeling a little lost and out of it, as people do who have entered into a circle to which they do not rightly belong. For though nobody had been rude to us or shown by look or word that we had trespassed, yet we could not but

feel that we were inferior beings—townsfolk—
and that, far from having inspired respect, we
had been looked upon as people whom it is
kinder to ignore. And then in the midst of
this depression who should come down upon us,
like a rescuing 'deus ex machina,' but our artist
friend, accompanied by a lady in Black Forest
dress, whom he introduced as Frau S——, *the*
person who could really tell us everything there
is to be known about the peasants and their
ways. At the same time he suggested that,
as there was yet two hours to dinner-time, it
would be a good idea to explore one of the
side valleys, unknown to the ordinary traveller,
and visit the distant 'Höfen' which lie hidden
in the recesses of the mountains. Glad of such
good and wise company, we crossed the bridge
and struck up westwards by a narrow footpath,
which wound its way pleasantly by the side
of the Schulzbach, whose sparkling waters come
tumbling down from the hills to meet the
mightier Gutach. And again it was a new
Black Forest which revealed itself to our eyes
—an idyllic country, half meadow, half forest,
a valley so narrow that it was scarcely more
than a deep dell, whose verdant green seemed
almost luminous contrasted with the background of pines and firs. And here and there,
hidden in some unexpected corner, a little farm,

or Gutle, as they are called, rose up out of the green, and some old peasant woman, left behind to prepare the Sunday dinner, nodded us a wondering good-day.

"For the most part there are only small land-owners round here," our guide told us as we turned to the left and mounted a steep path. "We call their cottages and grounds 'Gütle' to distinguish them from the big Bauern Hofen, one of which latter we shall see later on. Meanwhile, there is the Fuchs Loch Gütle and the Fuchs Loch Bauer."

We had now reached the top of the hill and discovered a small, picturesque, if rather tumbledown, cottage built up against the rising ground A very old man sat sunning himself in the porch, but he scarcely seemed to see us, and our questions were answered by a little bareheaded, barefooted boy who was watching over a herd of geese.

"The Fuchs Loch Bauer is ninety years old and very deaf," our guide remarked. "In all probability he will never come down into the village again, except when he is buried. And, indeed, he is no exception—a great many of these old peasants hardly ever come down into the village, or, if they do, look upon the journey as a great experience."

He then told us something of the ordinary

A VILLAGE FÊTE IN GUTACH

Black Forest peasant's life—a hard, joyless life
enough judged by our standards, but marked
throughout by quaint customs, which vary with
every village. As a rule a child is baptized
a few days after its birth, but in the interval
the Gutach folk take special precautions with
their newborn, it being absolutely for the child's
well-being that, from the ringing of the evening
bell till daybreak, a light should burn unin-
terruptedly at the cradle-side. And then, as
a special protection against evil, the unchristened
baby has crusts of bread given it, the boy
receiving that which is cut from the upper part
of the loaf, a girl from the lower half. In other
parts of the country, as in the neighbouring
Shapach Valley, the ceremonial of baptism is
accompanied by many and quaint rites. On
the road down to the church the friendly Höfen
salute the procession with gunshots—a form
of greeting distinctly royal, if rather disturbing
for the infant mind—and before entering the
church itself a short prayer is said. As a rule
—in Catholic regions—the baby receives the
name of the saint on whose day it is born, and
the ceremony of baptism having been performed,
it is taken by the Gotti (godmother), and
afterwards by the Gotti (godfather), for a sort
of processional walk round the altar. Then the
whole company betakes itself to the nearest

inn, where a feast in accordance with the wealth and position of the parents has been prepared. During the festivity the principal personage is laid in the so-called 'Herrgottswinkel' (a niche which is to be found in the corner of every Black Forest dwelling-room, and which usually contains the family Bible—hence the name), and it has happened that in the general merrymaking the unhappy cause has been altogether forgotten and eventually left behind on the return homewards. However, we will suppose that our imaginary baby has survived its baptism and the following three weeks, at the end of which time the Gotti pays a state visit to mother and child, bringing with her the customary presents of coffee, sugar, and bread, as well as a purse with one new silver piece, for the as yet unappreciative infant. At Christmas the Gottikleid (godmother's dress) is hung on the tree for the new member of the family, and with the child's first entry into school it receives the so-called Gottihut (hat) from its godmother. It very often happens that, until that first memorable day, the child never sees the face of any other children save those of its brothers and sisters; for the Hofen which lie in complete isolation on the mountains are like worlds in themselves, and in the long, stormy winter months the inhabitants are to

all intents and purposes cut off from their
fellow-creatures. At the age of six, however,
our particular protégé (for interest's sake I have
made him a boy) makes his first journey down
into the village and fights his first battles
with the German language 'as she is spoke'
in that particular region. From that hour the
hard and serious life begins. No matter what the
weather is, or what dangers from wind and storm
may threaten, he must twice a day cover the
sometimes considerable and tedious road which
divides homestead from village, and all that
with only the support of the roughest food and
clothed in the poorest garments. It is a case
of the survival of the fittest. Consequently,
if the boy survives these first rough years, he
is almost certain to develop into a strong,
hardy man, whereas weak, unhealthy children
succumb early to the kind but far from healthy
treatment which is customary amongst the
Black Forest people.

At the age of ten the boy is set to work,
either on his father's Hof or, if he be one of
many brothers, on some neighbouring farm,
where he acts as cowherd or stableboy. His
position is no sinecure. At four o'clock in the
morning he is already out of bed and helping
the head man in the stables; then there is a
hurried breakfast of broth and dry bread, of

which he partakes with the whole family round the table by the Herrgottswinkel. A silent meal this! Save for the prayer which precedes a general attack on the steaming bowl, no one speaks, and there is no sound save the clatter of spoons. Knives and forks are unknown to the ordinary Black Forest Bauer. His meat is cooked together with his soup, and for this rough, unchanging menu a wooden spoon is a quite sufficient weapon. The meal over, a general prayer is said at the open window, and our small friend departs with his mixed charge of oxen, cows, sheep, and goats. As it is summer he goes with the minimum amount of clothing—without hat or shoes or stockings—but with a hunk of bread in his pocket, a knife, and an enormous turnip-shaped watch, which is to tell him when the hour comes to return. For in the hot hours of the day the cattle must rest either in the stables or in the shade of the forest, and, moreover, by twelve o'clock the young cowherd must be in the village school with what learning he has managed to cram into his slow brain in between whiles. It must be admitted that his intelligence is of the kind that goes slowly but surely. Once he has learnt his lesson he is not likely to forget it, but the learning represents many a hard trial of patience for the much-worried Herr Dorf Lehrer (village schoolmaster). In any case, from the time the boy has become an independent worker, school matters have to take a secondary place in his day's programme. The school must even adapt its hour to the convenience of the scholar, and in harvest-time the master may be thankful if one or two of his more industrious pupils make their appearance at the odd times at their disposal. Fortunately, the Herr Lehrer is usually himself a Black Forester and, knowing the hardships of the peasant's life and the value of his harvest, is prepared to close an eye at such small irregularities. With the winter the cowherd's task is at an end, and he receives his wages—a pair of trousers, a waistcoat, and a pair of boots !—and he is free either to engage himself further for the rest of the year or to go home. We will suppose that he chooses the former course, and that, until his fourteenth year, he remains a servant at the big Hof where he made his first experiences. His fourteenth year marks a new period in his life. In the first place, his schooldays are over ; in the second, he is allowed on Easter Sunday to appear in the full glory of his 'Tracht.' From that day he must be accounted a man. But his manhood brings very little change. There is no great advancement possible for him, for high and low, rich and poor share the hard work with absolute impartiality, and the young cowherd is to all intents and purposes no worse off than his master. And so his life promises to be one of deadly, stunting monotony, and there is no doubt that our friend would become the dullest, most ignorant peasant on the earth's surface were it not for the one thing which stands before him as he approaches his twentieth year —his two years with the Army.

All the nonsense which has been talked respecting compulsory service must sink out of sight before the wonders which these two years perform for the German people—especially, perhaps, for the Black Forester. Decked with ribbons of the national and Badish colours, our young cowherd mounts the decorated wagon which is to carry him and his companions to the station. The village band accompanies him —amidst encouraging shouts he bids his village farewell and makes his first entry into the great unknown world. He enters an ignorant, uncouth lout, to whom the uses of such things as pocket-handkerchiefs, knives, and forks are unknown, slovenly, stooping with all the physical defects which result almost inevitably from his careless upbringing; he returns a trim young soldier, well set up, well fed, well clothed, his intellect brightened by contact with the world, his whole 'moral' raised by the two years of healthy discipline. Though he acknowledges that these years were the happiest he ever spent, he is none the less glad to return to his home and his people. And what stories he has to tell of his experiences in the manœuvres, of his first glimpse of his Emperor, who deigned to compliment *his* company on its particular smartness! And how eagerly he compares notes with his old father, who had served in *the* regiment through the grand years of 1870–72, and whose eyes still gleam when he hears that, as then, so to-day, the Army is ready to do and die for 'Kaiser und Reich!' So it is as a smart 'Reservist' that our cowherd returns, wearing as sign of his freedom the cap of his regiment, and bearing jauntily a walking-stick bedecked with ribbons. It speaks well for him that, in spite of all he has seen and done, he takes his part in the old life with unfaltering goodwill. By this time his father is too old to bear the brunt of the work, and so, as eldest son, he stays at home and prepares himself for the unwished-for day when he shall enter into full possession.

The lot of the eldest son in the Black Forest is not a happy one; he is treated as an integral part of the estate, and, no matter if he have talent or ambition, he is bound for life to the Hof—to a work which may be wholly distasteful to him. The other sons may go out into the world and make their way—as many of the Black Foresters have done—in trade, or even in art or literature, but he must remain, submitting absolutely to the iron law of custom which is handed down from father to son. He is free in nothing—not even in his marriage. Were he a prince his alliance could not be arranged with more regard for the 'convenances.' It may be that his affections are secretly given to the daughter of a neighbouring Bauer, but his affections and wishes count for nothing against the traditions of the family. The girl may be honest and good, but she is poor, her father's Gütle is heavily mortgaged, and the young man's people demand of him that he should marry wealth and position. *Noblesse oblige!* And so one day the young peasant puts on his best clothes and drives with his father to the Hof of the Gross Bauer whose daughter's *dot* is known to be a considerable one. There is very little love-making in the matter, as may be supposed. First of all the parents discuss the weather, the crops, etc., and then the real subject of interest is approached with great caution and delicacy. The Gross Bauer pretends that the idea of giving away his daughter so soon had never occurred to him, and the visitor pretends that he simply mentioned it *en passant,*

as it were. Then both sides, amidst much grunt-
ing and scratching of heads, agree that they
have no objection to the plan, and the eldest
daughter is called in. It may be that she is
both plain and unamiable, but as that merely
means that the *dot* will be increased by some
hundreds of marks, the father of the young
fellow is rather pleased than otherwise, and the
young fellow's feelings in the matter do not
count. Fortunately, very little is expected
of him. After the girl has shaken hands all
round and drunk the health of the guests, the
conversation proceeds about as follows :—

" Na, Madel, we want a Bure (wife) up at
our Hof. What do you think about it ? "

" It doesn't concern me," retorts the girl, with
a toss of her head.

" Well, we've come all this way to find out,
and don't want to go home without an answer.
Speak out—would you like it ? "

" You'd better settle it with father."

" Settled already. What have you to say ? "

" I'm willing if Michal is willing."

Thereupon the young peasant, who hitherto
has taken no part in the proceedings, is pushed
forward, and with as much heartiness as he can
muster, he invites her to visit the Hof on the
following Sunday, and the matter is settled. The
next Sunday, as arranged, the girl and her parents

arrive in state at the Hof, and whilst the fiancé
conducts her about the house and shows her the
kitchen which is to be her future domain, the
parents sit together and discuss the practical
sides of the case—that is to say, the marriage
settlement. As a rule, the village notary is
brought in to assist, and the matter is thrashed
out to a last farthing, for the Black Forester
is a cunning, hard-headed business man, and
when two peasants get together it is a case of
Greek meeting Greek. In the marriage settlement is included the bride's dowry, the value of
the Hof—which is now to pass into the eldest
son's hands—the share of his sisters and brothers,
and the amount to be set aside for the retiring
parents. Lastly, the wedding-day is fixed, and
by the time the young couple have returned
from their tour of inspection there is nothing
left for them to do but to say 'Amen' to the
arrangements made on their behalf. The next
matter is the sending out of invitations.
Although a public notice is usually put in the
papers, it is customary to send a woman—Ladfrau,
or invitation woman—from Hof to Hof, and as
she is always paid for the bringing of the invitation by presents of food, it often happens that
a poor couple does the inviting in person so
as to reap the reward. The invitation, which is
spoken, not written, runs as follows :—

A VILLAGE FÊTE IN GUTACH

"On Monday week you are politely requested to attend the marriage of the —— Michal [the surname or name of the Hof comes first] and the —— Marie. The church is at ten o'clock, and afterwards comes a visit to the inn. If we can help you in any way we shall always be glad to do so, whether it be in joy or sorrow—but let it be rather in joy."

The charm of the little formula lies in the dialect, with its quaint turns and abbreviations; but since the Black Forest dialect is sometimes not to be understood by the Germans themselves, I must fain translate into plain English.

A few days before the wedding the old couple make their solemn exit from the Hof, taking with them their other children and such possessions as they have reserved for themselves by the settlement. An adjoining house on the estate—the so-called 'Libtighus'—has been prepared for their reception, and this formal surrender of the reins into the younger's hands is looked upon as a right and natural course of events. As soon as the new master has entered into possession he has the old Hof scoured from top to bottom, in order that everything shall be in perfect condition by the time the bride's trousseau arrives. The trousseau is naturally an enormous affair and, save for the manner of its arrival, differs little from that of a town girl

with well-to-do parents. A fine new Leiterwagen (we have already encountered one of
these vehicles in Boll), drawn by four much-
beribboned horses, is packed with all the bride's
possessions, even to the marriage bed, which
crowns the whole grand collection in all the
splendour of its bright red covering.

On the eve of the wedding - day comes the
'Tschäpphirsch,' an unpronounceable ceremony,
which is to all intents and purposes the bride's
farewell to her home. The relations and friends
of both contracting parties are invited, and the
chief part of the meal is composed of a not
particularly appetising dish of pottage, to which
is attached a nosegay. If the bridegroom is
able to get hold of the flowers unhindered and
unobserved, he is supposed to have won the
mastery in his new home life, and on his having
successfully performed the feat, the bride is
presented by her mother and friends with
mottoes suitable for the occasion. The festivities
last until midnight, and as they begin again at
break of day, there is not much rest for the
inmates of either Höfen. Naturally, the whole
village takes part in the rejoicings. Already
with the rising of the sun the young people
begin to stream up to the respective homes of
the bride and bridegroom, where wine and cake
are to be had in unlimited quantities. Then

come the relations and friends, the village
musicians, the Militarverein (military union—a
a kind of association for all soldiers of the
Reserve, which is found in every village and
town in Germany, and to which our young
peasant naturally belongs). In fact, everybody
who is anybody makes an appearance and is
adorned with bright ribbons and nosegays.
Then, after a short prayer has been said, the
procession is got into order. First goes a young
cowherd, staggering under an enormous may
tree, then come the bridegroom's old military
comrades with drum and waving flags, then the
musicians, playing a wedding-march with all
the energy at their disposal, and, lastly, the
much-plagued bridegroom and the whole of his
mighty clan. Thus they reach the village,
where a pause is made, since the bride, with
feminine unpunctuality, has not yet put in an
appearance. Nothing is prettier than the scene
in a village street on such a peasant's wedding-
day. The profusion of flowers and gay ribbons,
the picturesque costumes, and the pretty, laughing faces of the womenfolk make a picture to
which the beauty of forest and mountain makes
a fitting background. At last the listeners hear
the sound of distant music, and soon afterwards,
amidst cries of welcome, the bride's procession
turns the corner of the street. She has had far

to come, so that this time the procession is a
mounted one. One Leiterwagen after another
draws up with its cargo of guests, relations, and
musicians, and whilst the bride, who has been
helped to alight by her future husband, runs
into a neighbouring house to adorn herself in
the 'Tracht' of his people (the costly dress is
one of his wedding presents to her), the procession orders itself anew. Again it is the cowherd with the may tree who leads the way, first
to the town hall, where the civil ceremony is
gone through, and then to the church. The
marriage service over, the bride with her
bridesmaids opens the so-called 'Opfergang'
round the altar, the men follow, and thus the
crowded church empties itself out into the sunlit street, and the serious part of the great day
is over. The newly married couple make their
first visit to the clergyman, who congratulates
them and in return receives an invitation to the
feast together with a bouquet from the bride.
Then the whole party adjourns to the chosen
Gasthaus, where the merrymaking begins. The
bride and bridegroom open the dance, and from
that moment all form and ceremony disappear.
Flower-sellers, women with cakes and various
dainties wander in and out amongst the guests,
who 'pay their way' and amuse themselves
after their own fashion until midnight strikes,

and the bride and bridegroom return to their home on the mountains.

Thus a wedding in the Black Forest is neither a small nor inexpensive affair, and though each district has its own peculiarities, the above method of procedure is fairly typical. In Gutach it is customary that the bridegroom should 'buy' the bride from the escort which brings her down to the church, and the young men who surround her make a hard bargain out of the business, so that the harassed bridegroom may think himself lucky if he gets off with no worse damages than a barrel or two of beer.

Not less ceremonious is the funeral, and since our Michal is a purely imaginary person, I hope I shall not be considered heartless if I hasten over his married happiness and endow him with a fatal illness. As soon as his condition is known, prayers are offered up daily by nine or ten boys and girls, deputed for the purpose, who afterwards receive presents as a reward for their efforts. Supposing the latter to have been in vain, the parish priest orders the special prayers to be said, and all the bells in the village are tolled, whilst relations and friends gather together in the house of mourning to pray and to wish the bereaved 'luck in sorrow'—a curious expression of consolation which may be taken as an allusion to the departed's future life, or

243

to the saying that sorrows never come singly—
in other words, as a wish that no more sorrow
may follow. Then the same people who usually
carry round the wedding invitations visit the
various neighbouring Höfen and request the
pleasure of the Bauern and their families' attend-
ance at the funeral and the subsequent dinner,
at the same time accepting the customary
presents with as woebegone a mien as possible
under the circumstances. A short time before
the actual funeral the coffin is carried outside
the house and surrounded by burning candles,
the relations say a last prayer, and then four
men belonging to the family raise the coffin on
their shoulders, and the melancholy, loudly
lamenting procession starts on its way down
to the village. The actual service differs little
from the usual ceremony, save that in some
parts of the country, as in Gutach, it is customary
for the masculine relations to keep on their
hats in church as a sign of mourning, and afterwards tastes differ as to holding or not holding
of the 'Leichenschmaus' (corpse feast, literally
translated). In sober, Protestant Gutach the
mourners retire quietly to their homes, but
elsewhere, I believe, the subsequent merrymaking strongly recalls an Irish wake, tempered,
no doubt, with a little German sentiment. At
one time Shapach had an unpleasant custom

COMING BACK FROM CHURCH, GUTACH.

of burying its dead without coffins. The village possessed a state coffin, which served for each dead person until his burial, when he was unceremoniously 'turned out' into his grave, covered with an old cloth, and buried without any further to-do. However, the State interfered, and now the good Shapachers are compelled to provide separate coffins—a piece of extravagance to which they at first strongly objected.

It would take volumes to describe the many and quaint customs to which the Black Forest Bauer still clings, for, as has been already said, each district has its own ways, and much depends on the predominating religion. Only one or two customs are common to most parts, such as the daily prayer at the open window, the origin of which practice is supposed to date from a time when the plague ravaged the whole country. The fear of infection made each Hof shut itself against its neighbour, and only the loud praying at the windows told that the inmates were still alive. Another explanation is that the devil and evil spirits have no power over the land so far as the sound of the praying is heard ; but, whatever the reason, the custom is very general.

Much of all this information we gained on our walk through the peaceful Loch (Loch

signifies hole, or small side valley), and by the
time we had reached our destination, the
Schlangenbauers' Hof, we felt that we already
knew something of its inmates, and were eager
to see them and their home from a more intimate
standpoint. Fortunately, our two friends were
well known, and our reception in the low-built
dwelling-room was of a most cordial character.
It was already dinner-time, but immediately the
whole family rose to greet us and expressed
their willingness to show the 'Fremden Damen'
everything that there was to be seen, though
the old father expressed his opinion that "surely
in England the cottages were much finer."

Rather curious was the intelligent interest
which the younger members took in my country
and its affairs generally. There were three
grown-up sons, fine-looking fellows in shirt
sleeves, who apparently disdained the use of
boots and stockings, but their manner would
have put many superior people to shame. They
were neither awkward nor shy, and, though
respectful, they behaved with the certain
indefinable ease and dignity which, nowhere
in the world more than in the Black Forest,
accompanies birth and breeding. For the
Schlangenbauer was a man of importance; his
Hof, one of the finest and most picturesque in
the whole country round, had been in the family

for generations, and in wealth—perhaps even
in ancestry—he probably outdid us all—and
probably he knew it. But not for a moment
were we allowed to feel that as townsfolk
without landed property we were on an inferior
social rung. At our request we were at once
introduced to the various points of interest
in the dwelling-room, as always, a square-built
apartment occupying a whole corner of the house.
Except in size—and in atmosphere—the Black
Forest Hofen differ very little from each other,
though their degrees of picturesqueness vary
with their age. The greater number have only
a 'ground floor,' but elevated so far from the
ground that a quite considerable flight of wooden
steps must be mounted before the visitor finds
himself in the dwelling-room—the only room,
sometimes, which deserves the name. The
interior is simple in the extreme, and I cannot
do better than take the Schlangenbauers' home
as an example. In the far corner, between the
two square-paned windows, was the Herrgottswinkel with the family Bible and the 'library,'
consisting of a few black-bound books; a rough
but well-scoured table occupied a place by the
wall; and a few chairs, together with an enormous
green porcelain stove, completed the furniture.
The stove was certainly the most important
feature; it occupied the whole of one corner and

was surrounded by a wooden bench, which, we were told, was the favourite sitting accommodation in the long and bitterly cold winter evenings.

"It does one good to put one's back against it after a long day's work," one of the sons observed, patting it affectionately; but I caught a faint pucker on Frau S——'s face which told volumes.

"You don't know what the atmosphere is like here in winter," she said in English, as we examined the military photographs which adorned the wooden walls. "The windows are tight shut, and the smoke is appalling. There are no chimneys, and when you add tobacco qualms to everything else, it is hardly possible to believe that a human being can breath in such air."

She then took us out into the passage, and pointed out the curious fact that in the whole building there was not a single nail or piece of iron. Everything was wood, and in places the riveting looked so loose and unsolid that it seemed as though the first storm would bring it crashing down. We expressed our doubts, but Frau S—— shook her head.

"A stone house could not be stronger, and the loose building is intentional. As there are no chimneys, there must be some outlet left for the smoke, which goes wandering about the house until it finds a cranny left for its escape."

"And what about fire?" we suggested dubiously.

Our companion shrugged her shoulders.

"When a fire does break out the place is lost," she admitted, "and the saddest part is that the cottages are never built up again in their original form. The peasants care nothing for the beauty of their homes and infinitely prefer the modern style, so that they are quite glad when a fire does break out." A rather suggestive smile broke over her face. "The Fire Insurance Companies are not fond of this department," she added, "and inquire very closely into the various cases. For, in spite of the apparent danger, it is not so easy for one of these cottages to catch fire. Look at this." She pointed to the ceiling of the kitchen, which we had just entered. "Everything is so thickly covered with hardened soot that the place is almost fireproof. If you try to break off a piece of this black stuff, you will find that it is as hard as iron."

We tried, and repressed a shudder at the thought of the ages of smoke-laden atmosphere which must have been necessary to have attained such a result.

"But the Black Forest people have the finest smoked hams in the world," our painter observed, with a friendly glance at the hooks hanging from the blackened ceiling. "You have no idea how good they taste after they have been left up there for a winter."

Frau S—— shook her head disapprovingly.

"The people pay for it with their lives very often," she said. "In spite of the wonderful climate, consumption is rife amongst the peasantry, and one of the chief causes is the atmosphere they live in. They have no idea of hygiene and, like most country people, have a strong objection to fresh air. But now come and look at the Tenne!"

The Tenne, or Heuboden, proved to be an enormous hayloft, whose existence we should never have expected from the front part of the cottage. Like all Black Forest Höfen the Schlangenbauers' home was built on rising ground, so that, whereas the front aspect was a comparatively large one, there was nothing to be seen from the back but the slanting thatched roof and the yawning entrance to the Heuboden. A rough track led up from the high-road, so that it was possible for a whole wagonful of hay to be driven into the loft and left there for the winter, if need be.

"In elegant houses, such as the Burgermeister's, they use the Heuboden for dancing," we were told, and since the loft covers the whole area of the house, we could well believe that it made an admirable ballroom.

From the Heuboden we were then taken to inspect the baking-oven—a tiny brick erection outside the house—but the pleasant smell of new bread reminded us that our own dinner-hour was at hand, and that the Gutach festivities were still before us. So we bade our amiable hosts farewell, and with many backward glances at the picturesque Hof, with its moss-grown roof and wooden beams and balconies dyed to a rich brown by wind and sunshine, we made our way homewards, satisfied that, if the Black Forest homesteads were the most lovely in the world to look on from the outside, the inside left much to be desired. No doubt everything was scrupulously clean and orderly, but our lungs were still full of the smoke and our eyes tingled uncomfortably, and a bright idea we had once fostered of taking a 'charming Black Forest cottage for next summer' died a natural death. On our way homewards Frau S——pointed out to us the Hofen which lay half hidden amongst the trees and gave us their various names.

"It is customary for the peasants to call themselves after their Hofen," she said. "Thus there is the Rotbauer, which simply means the peasant from the Rothof. His real name is quite different. I know them all," she added, with a merry laugh. "When I want eggs, as I do every day, I have to go from Hof to Hof and coax the people to sell me one or two. You have no idea how rare eggs and such things are in this part of the world."

By this time we had reached Gutach, and there parted company until the reunion at the Gemeindehaus in the afternoon. It was indeed a fête-day in the village. Everybody turned up in their best clothes—even the Schlangenbauer was there in all the glory of his red-lined velvet coat (I hope I shall not be considered boastful if I mention that he shook hands with us cordially)—and visitors poured in from Hornberg to see the exhibition of pictures by the two well-known Black Forest painters.

Amongst some of the sketches we discovered a delightful pen-and-ink portrait of the Lindenwirth, but the artist looked more alarmed than pleased at our congratulations.

"It was mad of me to exhibit it," he said in a whisper. "I forgot to ask the Lindenwirth's permission, and I hear he is terribly angry with me. It may be weeks before I am taken back into favour."

And, as a matter of fact, at that moment a burly figure loomed up in the doorway, and the culprit took to flight without so much as a 'good-day.' However, perhaps the copiously flowing beer and the general atmosphere of healthy gaiety helped to soothe him, for presently I heard him accepting the humbly tendered apologies with a gracious magnanimity. And it must have been a hardened heart that could have retained its bitterness on such an afternoon.

First there was a fairy play, acted and sung by the children under the stage management of a pretty schoolmistress in the Gutach 'Tracht'; and then came dancing on the green, climbing the greasy pole, sack-races, and all the other harmless amusements which go to make up a village fête. And the biggest part of all was played by the sun, who graciously condescended to shine cloudless from the moment of her rising to the hour when the gay crowd wandered homewards, making charming faces still more charming and lending forest and meadow a richer, brighter green. But let no one suppose that Frau Sonne's disappearance behind the mountains marked the close of the festivities. By the time we reached our Gasthaus the dining-room was already crowded, and no sooner was dinner over than chairs and tables vanished as though by magic, and old and young responded to the strains of the latest Gutach waltz (the 'Blue Danube,' I believe), as performed on the Lindenwirth's

piano by an obliging guest. We remained
spectators, for the Black Forest waltz is a
peculiar thing. The masculine partner puts
both arms round the lady's waist, and the
following proceedings resemble the lurchings
of a ship in a heavy sea rather than a waltz.
But apparently those concerned enjoyed themselves, and that, after all, was the chief thing.
Only the Herr Lindenwirth stood apart and
watched the gaily dressed peasants rotate
around him with a benignancy that was not
unmixed with disapproval.

"Much work they will do to-morrow!" he
remarked to us, as we stole away to the quiet
of our own rooms. But, alas! the quiet was
only comparative, for the morning hours were
well advanced before the hubbub of music and
laughter died away in the distance, and we were
compelled to admit—not altogether in the best
of tempers—that the Black Forester has a good
share of German thoroughness—especially in
the matter of amusing himself.

CHAPTER XIII

OVER RIPPOLDSAU AND THE KNIEBIS
TO BADEN-BADEN

EARLY the next morning we bade our friends
in Gutach farewell, and with a last glance at
our luggage, which we were not to see again for
many days, we mounted our bicycles and rode in
high spirits out of the apparently sleeping village.

"Positively, I believe we are the only people
awake!" my German friend remarked, with the
pharisaical pride of the early riser. "How
can people stay in bed on such a lovely
morning! I suppose the good folk have not
got over the effects of last night."

On the outskirts of the village we found that
at least one person was awake and on foot
besides our energetic selves. Frau S——, still
dressed in her dainty 'Tracht,' awaited us at
the crossing and presented us with a welcome
gift of the most delicious peaches, gathered, as
she told us, from her own walls.

"They will help you over the dusty road,"

she said. "You have a hot day before you, and I think you would have been wiser if you had done as the villagers do and got the worst part of your day's work over before ten o'clock."

"The villagers," said my friend, with dignity, "are not so much as awake even."

Frau S—— laughed her laugh of superior wisdom.

"I warrant you there is not an able-bodied man or woman or child who was not up and about hours ago," she said—"only they are not in the village. You will see them at work in the fields. The Black Forester is no idler."

Her prophecy verified itself, for as we left Gutach behind us and wheeled our way leisurely along the smooth and level road, we saw to the right and left of us the bowed figures of the workers, who looked up as we passed them to exchange a friendly 'Tag.' From their flushed faces we judged that already many hours of work lay behind them, and our self-satisfaction dwindled. Men and women toiled side by side, and as we saw how the latter bore their share, we no longer wondered at the few *middle-aged women* we had seen in our wanderings. To all appearances there are no middle-aged women. There are children, whose beauty, especially in and about Gutach, makes them a positive feature of the place, and there are charming, rosy-cheeked

BLACK FOREST COTTAGE.

girls, but from the moment that she marries the Black Forest woman loses both youth and beauty. Child-bearing, coupled with the inevitable toil in the fields, does its work, and the pretty, fresh-complexioned girl shrivels in a few years to a bent and haggard old woman. I have said the field-work is inevitable, and, indeed, it is so; for though some of the peasants have amassed considerable wealth it has only been at the price of unrelenting labour, in which every one has taken his share, and, moreover, for one 'Grossbauer' there are dozens of day-labourers who have to fight unremittingly for their existence. In this fight the wife bears her part as a matter of course, and without complaint. She teaches her children to watch over each other whilst she works with her husband in the fields, and as soon as they have the strength they too join in the general activity. As Frau S—— said, the Black Forester is no idler, and the price which he pays for the right to live is a heavy one. In the summer there are the fields to tend, and in autumn and winter comes the dangerous wood-cutting on the high mountains. How dangerous the latter occupation is may be judged by the fact that the cost of a tree bought on the mountain is less than half that of the same tree in the valley. And it is not strange that it should be so, for its headlong course down the narrow frozen cuttings, or later in the year on the breast of some swollen torrent, represents an ever-constant and inevitable danger for the hardy wood-feller. But the Black Forester is something more than a mere labourer, he is also an artist with deft fingers and an eye for colour, as the pretty pottery and the handsome carved clocks testify. Show me the traveller who has successfully wandered through the Black Forest without collecting cuckoo clocks of all sizes and dimensions, or the South German whose house does not echo hourly with the plaintive voice of a make-believe cuckoo! Personally, I confess to a hopeless weakness for these quaint and most reliable timepieces. There is something about them so simple, honest, and homely that I think they must have absorbed something of the spirit of their makers who laboured at them in the long winter evenings on the mountains. Their tick is the most soothing sound in the world, and when they *do* go wrong, which is seldom, there is always the satisfaction that one can go plunging about their works with amateurish zeal without inflicting irremediable damage.

But to return to our travels. As the reader will have judged by a previous remark concerning our luggage, we had once more yielded to the deceitful fascinations of the knapsack, and, forgetful of our painful experiences on the Feldberg, had loaded our backs with sufficient necessities for a three days' genuine ramble. For we were now entering on the North Black Forest, and in our wanderings over the heights of the Kniebis and the Hornisgrinde there was no railway to help us, and even our bicycles were destined to be left to the mercies of the Rippoldsau hotel porter. It was a case of a long stretch of strict pedestrianism, and, thanks to the optimism which comes with sunshine and fresh morning air, we faced the prospect with all good courage.

In the meantime our road through the broad and lovely valley left nothing to be desired. Peaceful villages, cheerful meadows, and picturesque Hofen greeted us on our level way, and every now and again a passing peasant woman in her workaday Tracht brought us and our cameras into a state of mild excitement. For it is a delicate matter, this photographing of the peasant folk. They are shy, suspicious, and proud, and we had long since arranged a small comedy which gave us an opportunity without wounding their feelings—namely, as soon as we caught sight of an interesting 'subject' coming in our direction, we dismounted, one of us posed gracefully at the side of the road, and whilst our victim passed by with the soothing conviction that we were engaged in making 'souvenirs' of each other the wicked deed was done. At first we were uneasy as to the 'fairness' of the proceedings, but photographers are notoriously conscienceless, and since all great people must submit to the impertinences of the kodak fiend I hope our Black Forest friends will forgive us—if they ever find us out, which is hardly likely.

With these welcome interruptions we passed Hausach and Wolfach, and hailed, not without disappointment, the first signs that we were approaching the great Rippoldsau Bad, the most popular of all the Kniebis watering-places. The signs were, indeed, such that we were glad that our plans only allowed for dinner and a few hours' rest before we proceeded on foot to the Kniebis itself. Heavily laden motor-cars, luggage-wagons, and well-dressed folk leisurely strolling back to their table d'hôte dinners met us on the road, and long before we dismounted at the doors of the Kurhaus Hotel we were prepared for another St. Blasien. But Rippoldsau proved less of a disappointment than we had at first feared. In spite of the bazaars and the baths and the Kur guests lounging about in hammocks and long chairs in every corner, in spite of the objectionable motor-cars which every two hours

came up with fresh visitors from Wolfach, in
spite of the general air of rather tawdry
smartness, Rippoldsau remains one of the most
beautiful spots in the Northern Black Forest.
At the foot of the great Kniebis, it is surrounded
by pine-covered mountains whose grandeur is
yet softened by an idyllic peace and loveliness.
There are no wild gorges and rocky valleys here;
it is a world to itself, closed in and almost
mysterious, as though it lay under some fairy
charm, and all the unpleasant additions, such
as human beings and motor-cars, appear very
much in the light of gnomes and goblins who
have intruded into a country of fair, invisible
spirits Unfortunately in the summer the
gnomes have decidedly the upper hand. They
crowd out all poesie and charm, and beautiful
Rippoldsau, with its healing waters, becomes
a rather stuffy and overcrowded popular resort
for the well-to-do middle-class—a very middle
class sometimes, be it said with regret. But
in late spring and early summer the Black
Forest has no lovelier spot to show, and, with
the exceptions of Badenweiler and Baden-Baden,
no finer hotels.

The new Sommerau Hotel, situated a little
above the village, though not large, can stand
comparison, as far as luxury and tastefulness
of decoration are concerned, with any hotel in

Europe; and though the prices are higher than is usual in the Black Forest, yet the visitor has at least the satisfaction of knowing that he is getting something for his money. The mineral baths are highly valued by the medical faculty, and thus quite early in the year Rippoldsau opens its doors to those seeking quiet and health in peaceful, sheltered surroundings. Already in the fifteenth century the efficacy of the waters was known and valued, but as usual in the more remote parts of the Black Forest a monastery was the first building to be erected, and although it suffered with the rest of Rippoldsau when, in 1643, it was attacked by the Swedes, it still exists in a modernised form and serves the village as church as well as a 'Sehenswürdigkeit,' as the German guide-books say. But the heat of midday—and the midday heat in Rippoldsau can be almost tropical— prevented us from paying the historical spot a visit, and four o'clock saw us already attacking the ascent of the Kniebis. *Bien entendu* our bicycles had been sent to join our luggage at Wolfach, and our well-filled knapsacks were all that was left us; but by the time we had reached our destination we found that even they were more than we liked. Still, it would be un- grateful to complain, for the walk to the highest point of the Kniebis, the Alexander-

RIPPOLDSAU.

schanze, in the cool of the summer's evening, remains in our memory as one of the most beautiful of all our rambles. The Kniebis, though it needs 600 feet to make it the equal of the Hornisgrinde, is none the less the most important mountain range of the Northern Black Forest, and forms a kind of watershed between north and south. The Hornisgrinde, in spite of its more pretentious aspect, is no more than an outrunner of the massive Kniebis, whose geological character has made it, from the Roman ages onwards, a great pass between the Rhine and Neckar Valley. Cut on either side by deep valleys and ravines, the Kniebis represents a broad comb of moorland, almost entirely free from the wild, impenetrable forest growth which in ancient days made the traversing of the mountains a dangerous, almost impossible task. Yet an actual Roman high-road does not seem to have existed, and to this very day the Kniebis is one of the least populated mountains. The terrific storms which threaten it in winter and the unfertile nature of the soil are indeed sufficient reasons for the latter fact, and to make up for the deficiency, if deficiency it be, the Kniebis bears proof enough of its importance as a strategical pass in the three great entrenchments which defend its summit. We came upon the first of these, the Alexanderschanze, after two hours' walking, and a comfortable inn offering us accommodation, we decided to spend a night in the refreshing cool of the mountains, doubly grateful after the heat of the valley. On our way we had passed the one important colony of which the Kniebis can boast, a village bearing the same name but of comparatively recent origin, having been founded somewhere at the beginning of the nineteenth century. To this day the inhabitants have retained something of their original patriarchal character; they form one family and speak a dialect which has no resemblance to that of the valleys beneath, and if an old chronicle speaks truth of them their ancestors, though of a good-natured and simple character, were not noted for their respect for the rights of property. By this time, however, this unfortunate weakness has no doubt passed away, and if one may judge from appearances the inhabitants may be wholly trusted with the life and property of the travellers who seek lodging in their midst. For our part, we had wandered farther simply because the beauty of the evening tempted us to greater pedestrian efforts, and not at all because of the probably libellous insinuations of an irresponsible old chronicler. For the rest, the straggling village offers an example of the divided religious and political state which is rather characteristic of the Black

RIPPOLDSAU, ANOTHER VIEW.

Forest, one half being Badish and Catholic and the other half Württembergisch and Protestant; but the times of strife are past, and the two confessions appear to agree admirably together.

After a comfortable night spent in the Gasthaus zur Alexanderschanze we spent the first half-hour of the morning inspecting the remains of the entrenchments which in 1734 were erected by the Duke Alexander of Württemberg against the inroads of the French armies. Altogether, like so many other mountains of the Black Forest, the Kniebis has seen stormy times, and after half an hour's walking over the open moorland we came across the second remains of warlike days. The Schwaben, or Röschenschanzen, as the entrenchments are called, were built in 1769 by a Major Rösch of the Württembergischen army as a barrier across the path of the French soldiers crossing the mountain from the Renchthal. Unfortunately a traitorous peasant betrayed a secret pass to the enemy, and the defenders, taken by surprise, were driven out at the point of the bayonet.

Two minutes' walk farther on brought us to the ruins of a third place of defence, the Schwedenschanzen, but their origin is veiled in mystery. It is supposed that they date from the Thirty Years' War, and were built by the same Swedes who afterwards became the terror of Rippoldsau, and hence the name 'Schweden' was given to them; but of the entrenchments, as well as of their history, little remains. From these last ruins our road lay through a stretch of uninterrupted loneliness, but never for a moment were we left in doubt as to the correctness of our route. At every turn we were met by multitudinous signposts which sternly directed us to the 'right road,' and though well provided with maps and guidebooks we found that we had no need of them. Thus, gradually descending, we left the open heights of the Kniebis behind us and plunged into the cool shadow of the Forest. Already the peculiar charm of these northern regions was beginning to creep over us; there is, indeed, a scarcely describable 'something' about the Northern Black Forest which makes the traveller, who has heard so much concerning the superiority of the south, wonder where the critics had their eyes and critical faculties. The explanation is, no doubt, that the area of the Northern Black Forest is smaller, and the really beautiful region limited to the eastern confines with the Kniebis and the Hornisgrinde. The valleys which lie westwards, though charming in their peaceful way, have nothing to offer in comparison with the valleys of the south. They lack grandeur and also the marked characteristics lent them by their inhabitants. In the north the 'Trachten' have almost entirely disappeared, the picturesque thatched cottages have given place to bricks and mortar, and people and villages have sunk to the dead level of uniformity which is the penalty of modern civilisation. But in such places as Allerheiligen, where our three hours' wandering brought us, the magic beauty of the Black Forest finds its final, perhaps its most perfect, expression. The moderate-sized Gasthaus is the only dwelling for miles around; it lies high up on the mountain-side in a kind of dell, so closed in by the surrounding pine-covered summits that the wanderer feels he must be in the heart of a valley, yet blown with such fresh and invigorating air that the heat and depression which he has brought with him from the lowlands passes as though touched by some health-giving magician's wand. It seemed to us, as we stood on the path which winds its way downwards to the hotel, that the green of the pines and firs was richer and deeper than anywhere else: the very air, in spite of the midday sun, was full of the vigour of spring, an eternal youth seemed to breathe out of the silence, broken only by the thunder of the distant water-fall, and the ruins lying close to the hotel forgot their age and took on an appearance of being simply an architectural addition to the young world about them. Perhaps on account of a direct disregard of a heavenly sign, the old monastery was noted for its misfortunes. In 1196, the year in which the Countess Uta von Calw determined to lay the first stone, a donkey, laden with the gold which was to pay for the building, struck a certain rock with its hoof and immediately a spring made its appearance, proving beyond doubt that this was the spot chosen by heaven for the site of the monastery. If the wanderer doubts this story he need only follow a narrow pathway leading westwards from the monastery garden, and he will find the spring itself—called the 'Eselsbrunnen'—with an inscription which should put his unbelief to shame.

Unfortunately the spirit of doubt seems also to have possessed the Countess, for with womanly determination — or obstinacy, as her masculine critics would say—she clung to the site she had chosen, in defiance of all signs and wonders, so of course the monastery fared badly. It was more than once burned to the ground, its abbots were expelled, imprisoned, and occasionally murdered, until at last in 1803 it was finally suspended. Even then the angry heavens were not satisfied, for no sooner had the monks taken their departure than a stroke of lightning

ALLERHEILIGEN.

reduced the building to its present state of ruin, and since then it has only served as an ornament for the surrounding country. Still, we cannot blame the good Countess, for her choice of site could scarcely have been bettered, and the donkey's action must be regarded as the result of a contrary and contradictory spirit. For it is not alone the peaceful surrounding forest which makes Allerheiligen famous and beloved; there is the waterfall—surely the most perfect and the most worthy of its reputation of all the many rivals which the Black Forest has to show. This is no tamed and decorated waterfall decked out to suit the taste of the tasteless. From a height of over three hundred feet the silver waters of the Grindenbach pour down through the narrow cleft in the mountain, foaming over seven falls, each of which has its own particular character and beauty. The path at its side, though safe and easy, shares the general appearance of rugged grandeur; it leads between mighty rocks, sometimes over the falls themselves, and nothing is more lovely than the view from one of these daringly constructed bridges, directly beneath the white volume of hurrying water, and in front a sudden opening out of the landscape, a wonderful glimpse of the distant world which in Allerheiligen the traveller seems to have left for ever behind him. Many strange, half-historical, half-legendary stories are told of the rocks over which the Grindenbach seeks its way to the valley, and many of them have received a name in accordance with their past. Two of the names, the 'Rabennest' (the Ravens' Nest) and the 'Zigeunerhohle' (Gipsies' Cave), are linked together. The latter place, a dark, in-hospitable-looking hole in the rock, once sheltered a troop of gipsies, one of whom, a beautiful girl, excited the love and admiration of a scholar at the monastery, a certain youth of the name of Lucas. As a sign of his devotion, the young man presented her with a ring which was supposed to bring luck to the owner so long as it remained in his keeping, but whose loss heralded dire misfortune. And, alas! one day as the gipsy maiden was preparing herself for a meeting with her lover, she foolishly laid the precious jewel aside, and a raven, attracted by the glitter, seized upon it and bore it to its nest on the precipice above the waterfall. The lamentations of the young girl determined Lucas to a daring attempt to recover the ring, and aided by two companions he let himself down by a rope into the depths, whither the raven had taken its plunder. Swinging peril-ously backwards and forwards, he was about to snatch the jewel from the nest, when, to the horror of the onlookers, the rope snapped and his body fell, crashing from rock to rock, down into the torrent beneath. From that moment the place became an object of suspicious dread, and at nights the scream of the unhappy gipsy girl can still be heard above the hoarse cry of the raven as it flies upwards from its nest among the rocks Altogether it is a curious fact, and perhaps it testifies to the extraordinary *romantic* beauty of the Northern Black Forest, that the regions north of the Kniebis team with legends, whereas the south can boast of but few, and those only of a scanty nature. It would take a volume to relate even the most important, and I restrict myself to those which concern the places of our wanderings.

Thus the day following saw us on our way to the so-called 'Edelfrauengrab' (Grave of the Noblewoman), which forms part of the Gottschlag waterfall. A very modest little waterfall this, scarcely more than a stream, whose course lies over a few boulders, but wholly charming, and best suited to the valley through which it winds its way. At first following the broad high-road behind Allerheiligen, we obeyed the behests of the signposts and entered upon a narrow path which led down to the left and in easy curves descended to the valley. There we discovered the Gottschlägbach and its waterfall—the latter needed some discovering—but it was some time

before we could make up our minds which of
the many likely-looking places marked the spot
where the unfortunate noblewoman had been
put to death. My companion settled on six
successive spots which were beyond all doubt
'it'; but at length a deep cave, in which the
waters of the fall churned themselves into a
white fury before continuing on their way, put
all former pretenders in the background. This
was unquestionably the 'grave,' and whilst I
endeavoured to take photographs from the
grassy mound opposite, my friend, to make good
former errors of judgment, related the true and
exact story of the Frau von Bosenstein. This
lady, the wife of the Lord of Bosenstein, whose
castle once guarded a neighbouring height, was
noted for her love of luxury, but above all for
her hard-heartedness and cruelty towards the
peasants on her land. Thus, one day during a
grand feast a poor woman came to the gates of
the castle and begged for food for herself and
her starving children. The Frau von Bosenstein
answered her with the remark that poor folk
should do without families, and refused her the
slightest assistance. The desperate woman thereupon raised her hand in malediction. "I go,"
she is reported to have said, "but God will
surely punish you, and I pray to Him that He
may curse you with seven children at one birth !"

The guests laughed the angry beggar to scorn, but shortly afterwards her prayer was answered, and the Frau von Bosenstein gave birth to seven healthy sons. Her anger and the dread of the mockery of her friends may be imagined, and since her husband was absent, she determined to rid herself secretly of at least six of the unwished offspring. Accordingly she gave them into the hands of an old woman, with the order that she should drown them in the stream below the castle. The servant was about to obey her mistress's command when she was startled by the arrival of Herr von Bosenstein himself, and in her endeavour to hide the babies in her apron she drew his surprised attention on herself, and he approached her with the request that she should tell him what she was concealing.

"Young puppies, sir," she answered, trembling. Whereupon the suspicious knight tore open her apron and discovering the children forced her to a confession. With the promise that if she kept silence he would spare her life, he took the babies from her and distributed them among the good people of the village, and for seven years his wicked wife lived in the belief that her deed had passed undiscovered and unpunished. But the day of retribution was to dawn. On the anniversary of his dread discovery, Herr von Bosenstein called an assembly of friends, and during the feast he asked his wife what punishment she would assign to a woman who wilfully had brought about the death of her own children. The unsuspecting woman answered that she would have her buried alive with a loaf of bread and a pitcher of water; and no sooner had she spoken her judgment than the door of the hall was thrown open and six young boys entered and made their obeisance.

"These are the children whom you would have murdered seven years ago!" thundered the enraged knight. "You have pronounced your own sentence." And heedless of her tears and entreaties, the unfeeling mother was conducted to the cave by the waterfall, and with the consolation of a crucifix, a loaf of bread, and a pitcher of water, there incarcerated to await a lonely and terrible death. The story, which reminded me a little of a certain well-known fairy tale, is proved not only by the ghost of the unrepentant Edelfrau, which haunts the scene of her execution, but by the curious recurrence of the name 'Hund' (dog) amongst the people of the district, who are supposed to be the descendants of the six children. In spite of its ghostly and unpleasant history, the Edelfrauengrab is a lovely spot overshadowed with green foliage, and, with its clear stream and miniature waterfall, a pleasant resting-place

for the wanderer ere he retraces his steps along
the gravel pathway which leads up into the
mountains. For those seeking the valley and
the railway Ottenhöfen lies half an hour's
walk away, but our intention being to cross
the Hornisgrinde to Baden-Baden we returned
the way we had come until we once more
attained the high-road, when, turning northwards, we reached Ruhstein after a two hours'
walk.

Of all places in the Northern Black Forest
the Ruhstein is the loneliest, perhaps on that
account the most beautiful. As its name testifies, it is no more than a small rocky plateau,
situated in the heart of the forest, five miles
from anywhere, with one solitary Gasthaus to
mark the spot and offer the weary traveller
food and lodging. Here we took up our
quarters for the night, for the climb from
Edelfrauengrab had been more than we had
anticipated, and, moreover, the deep peace of
the surroundings tempted us. We were now
on the frontier between Württemberg and Baden,
and two brightly painted posts, bearing the
arms of the two states, marked the invisible
border line. Ruhstein belongs—by a hair-
breadth, so to speak—to Baden, which state,
indeed (with the exception of Wildbad and
Herrenalb), possesses all the beautiful parts of

the Black Forest, and is famous both as a winter
and as a summer resort. Unpretentious but
comfortable, the hotel offers everything that
can be desired by moderate travellers—including
moderate prices—and the nature of the surrounding country makes it an admirable spot
for a lengthy stay. The land is wholly un-
cultivated, and the rambler is thus free to
wander where he will, as free and unhindered
as though the whole country belonged to him.
In bad weather there are the long, level
high-roads, which, even after the worst spells,
remain passable; on overclouded days there
are lovely stretches of open moorland, and
when the sun deigns to shine the forest paths
open their cool shade in every direction which
the traveller may fancy. Like all Black Forest
resorts, the Gasthaus is often overcrowded in
the high season; but here the loneliness is so
extreme, the forest-land so wide and sweeping,
that the guests seem to lose themselves in
its depths, and the feeling of being suffocated
by one's fellow-creatures, as is the case in
St. Blasien and Rippoldsau, is wholly absent.
But though Ruhstein offered so many temptations, we were too much under the influence
of our knapsacks and their limited though
heavy contents to linger, and the next day
we started northwards for the summit of the

Hornisgrinde, the highest mountain of the Northern Black Forest (3498 feet).

From our starting-point—already 2748 feet —the ascent was easy, and after twenty-five minutes we caught sight of the dark Wildsee lying beneath us like a sombre eye gleaming out of the forest. Unlike the Feldsee, no mighty precipices rise up around its edge, but it has none the less a gloomy fascination of its own, and we needed no one to tell us of the water-nymphs who in past times tempted infatu-ated shepherds to their destruction in the black, unfathomable waters. Virgin forests grow up to the water's edge, no woodman's axe ever rings in the profound silence : as throughout the ages so now the Wildsee lies in the midst of its jungle world, undisturbed and over-shadowed by its impenetrable mystery. Few wanderers ever descend to the water's edge, and we, too, contented ourselves with the view from the road above before continuing slowly on our way to the next and best known lake of the Northern Black Forest—the Mummelsee. An hour and a half's walk brought us in sight of the Hornisgrinde Tower, and already a fine view over the Rhine Valley, with the Strassburg Cathedral and the distant Vosges, rewarded us for our pains. But the much-prized Mummelsee disappointed us. No district in the Black Forest boasts of as many legends, and, indeed, in past ages, when the forest around knew neither tourist nor hotel-keeper, one can well imagine that the solemn shadows stirred the imagination of the huntsman whose prey led him to the water's edge, or of the adventurous shepherd tempted by stories of beautiful nymphs and fairies. 'Mummel' is supposed to be the name of the 'vermummten' (disguised) spirit which haunts the neighbourhood, and whose daughters, the 'Mummelchen' dwell in the depths of the waters. From the stories that are told of them they seem to have been as tender-hearted as they were beautiful, and unlike most of their race to have loved passionately and faithfully. But, alas,! their father, the stern old water-spirit, could be unrelenting in his severity, and one fair nymph, having so far forgotten his behests as to linger after midnight with her human lover, was torn away from him, and only a bloody stain on the face of the lake showed where she had met her punishment. The knight, who had honourably intended to wed his mysterious water-bride, shared the fate of an unhappy shepherd lad. The latter had ventured to call his nymph by name, and instantly a terrific storm broke over the lake, bloodstains rose to the surface, and the lady was never seen again. Presumably the old

'Mummel' had heard the amorous callings and had inflicted the death - penalty on his disobedient daughter. At any rate the shepherd, like his knightly predecessor, went mad with grief and hid himself as a hermit near the waterfall in Allerheiligen, speaking to no man and forgotten by the world.

Other similar stories are told of the water's inhabitants, but for many years the nymphs have remained in their undiscovered hiding-places, and one cannot altogether blame them. The modern tourist is scarcely calculated to awaken tenderness in the hearts of lovely water-spirits, accustomed to the homage of gorgeous knights and picturesque shepherd lads, and even if a Lohengrin made his appearance, I doubt if they would ever sufficiently overcome their disgust at the absurd boats and canoes which adorn (?) the lake, to rise to greet him. In a word, the Mummelsee suffers from its popularity. The whole charm must have once lain in its mystery and solitude, but rowing-boats, signposts, hotels, and the general *va-et-vient* have robbed it of all that, and the lake has not the majesty of the Feldsee to raise it above the degrading influence of admirers. Still, it is ungrateful to rail at the existence of the hotel (Gasthaus zum Mummelsee), for without the accommodation

our visit to the Hornisgrinde from the Ruhstein would have been beset with discomforts.
As it was, we could cast aside our burdens,
and, with the prospect of a good night's rest
before starting on our long march to Hundseck,
allow ourselves the pleasure of a leisurely survey
of the Hornisgrinde from its summit. A good
half-hour's somewhat stiff climbing brought us
to the four-cornered tower which marks the
highest point of the mountain, and from thence
we obtained an extended view over the Rhine
Valley to the west, and to the east over an uninterrupted, monotonous stretch of forest. The name
Hornisgrinde is derived from two words 'Hornis'
and 'Grinde,' but only the latter can be safely
traced back to its origin. In old German it was
a somewhat contemptuous term for 'head,' and
it is presumed that 'Hornis' means 'horn,' and
the adjective certainly suits well enough to be
accepted. For nearly an hour's walk the bald,
rocky mountain ridge stretches from north to
south, falling abruptly to the west in steep,
scantily covered cliffs, to the east in more gradual
slopes. The extreme barrenness of the Hornisgrinde is due, not to its height, but to the
marshy character of its formation, which permits
only a rough growth of turf, and wild, sometimes
rare and interesting, flowers. Here and there a
block of sandstone recalls its original covering,

and from its geological, as well as from its botanical standpoint, the Hornisgrinde is perhaps the most interesting mountain of the Black Forest. But it marks the beginning of that region which has laid the Black Forest open to the charge of being monotonous and depressing. Never without a certain charm, the road northwards lacks, nevertheless, the variety of the south. Endless forests of pine and fir lie behind and before, and though pleasant enough we found our seven hours' tramp over the Hornisgrinde to the hotel at Hundseck somewhat long and tedious.

Since the road is a very lonely one we had made ourselves entirely independent of wayside inns by taking our provender with us, thereby considerably adding to our load. This additional burden quickly disappeared, however, and thanks to occasional rests at such points where a gap in the wall of pine allowed us a free view of the valley, we reached Hundseck by way of the Mannheimer Strasse, over the Riesen and Hochkopf, in very fair condition. Unfortunately we had again to suffer for our habit of leaving our arrival unannounced, and in the already overcrowded hotel had to content ourselves with what accommodation a worried but still affable host managed to procure for us. Altogether we were compelled to write Hundseck down as one of those places better avoided in the high season. It lies too close to Karlsruhe, Mannheim, and Frankfurt not to be overrun with towns-folk seeking a cheap, not too distant summer resort. The air is good, the hotel comfortable in an unpretentious way, and Baden-Baden is easily attained by means of the dangerous-looking motor-cars, whose descent by the steep, sharply curving road must be the last thing in hair-raising excitements for the closely packed inmates. Altogether Hundseck is too popular. It is impossible to lose sight of the guests for more than five minutes at a time, and the unfortunate seeker after rest and peace finds himself constantly stumbling over one of the uncountable crowd of children who are ' up for the holidays.' Added to all this is the fact that in the high summer Hundseck and its surroundings are somewhat monotonous, and in spite of the beautiful pine forest and the lovely glimpse over the Rhine Valley the visitor soon wearies. In late summer, or late spring, or even in winter, when the serving-girls are less overworked (no genuine Black Forest hotel boasts of waiters, and I have found that, on the whole, girls are quicker, less over-bearing, less conscious of their superiority, and more obliging), Hundseck is an agreeable health

GEROLDSAU WATERFALL.

resort, especially for those who have not time to penetrate deeper. The same criticism can be applied to the neighbouring Sand and Plattig, which lie on the high-road to Baden-Baden at about half an hour's distance from each other; but the traveller, having got so far, is advised to seek quarters at the highest situated of the three, namely, Hundseck, and if he come at the right time of the year he will not be disappointed, either in the kindly welcome of his host or in the peace of his surroundings. But for us the season was already too far advanced, and having decided that if we had to have a crowd we would rather have a smart one, we packed up our goods and chattels, and early the next morning started downhill for Baden-Baden *via* Sand, Plattig, the Geroldsauer Waterfall, and lastly the justly famous, but for weary limbs rather lengthy Lichtenthaler Allée. The walk is thoroughly worth the exertion, and a good if rather expensive meal at the little restaurant by the waterfall makes a pleasant break before the pedestrian starts on the more wearying walk through the valley. At any rate, the tour on foot has the advantage of being perfectly safe, which is more than can be said of the motor service, and at our weariest moments we felt no envy for the heated, nervous-looking inmates

283

of the car as it went grinding and groaning round the scarcely negotiable curves. Tired, but entirely pleased with our long wanderings, and smugly self-satisfied at our prowess, we reached Baden-Baden, and at the quiet but comfortable hotel, Hirsch, reclaimed our luggage with the heartfelt joy which only those can feel who have existed for days on the contents of a lady's knapsack!

CHAPTER XIV

BADEN-BADEN AND SURROUNDINGS

WE were in the right mood for Baden-Baden, for at the bottom of our hearts we are both town children, loving the life and colour and brilliancy of the great world. Many days had passed since we had bidden Badenweiler fare-well. Though the long, solitary rambles through the forests and over the mountains remained a lovely, unforgettable memory, we could not but feel delight as, once more clothed in—comparatively—fashionable garb, we wandered about the streets of the town, breathing again, as it were, our natural air. 'The Queen of watering-places!' Objectionable term, suggest-ing trippers, and all the thereto connected horrors of cheap hotels, cheap amusements and excursions! And yet Baden-Baden deserves the title, given with all due respect and solemnity, as no other place in Germany, nay, in Europe, deserves it. Where else in the world is to be found so much true elegance, refinement, so much true, light-hearted amusement so closely linked with the most lovely world that Dame Nature ever created in a tender mood! No doubt it is a frivolous place this Baden-Baden. *On s'amuse* from early morn till late at night—there is nothing else to do. Frivolity, gaiety of the lightest, frothiest kind impregnates the very air with a sweet, sorrow-numbing perfume, and even the saddest, even those who have come to seek' lost health in the healing waters, soon throw aside sorrow and pain and take their share of life with the rest. Yet it is the most peaceful place in the world. The gaiety is so quiet, so masked with the reserve of those to whom pleasure is the natural element, that the most sensitive never realises in what a whirl of distractions he is living. There is none of the vulgar ' look-at-me-how-I-am-enjoying-myself' pleasure-seeking of such places as St. Blasien and Rippoldsau. Here the richest and most cultured of all the great nations meet and vie with each other, but without noise, without commotion. One wanders through the lovely Lichtenthaler Allée with the feeling that one has been transported into a magic world where everything ugly has been exterminated, even to the vice of an exaggerated, ostentatious luxury. *Bien entendu* there are exceptions, and short

periods when the exceptions are rife, as in the
great race week in August; but the visitor in
June or early July will find nothing to offend
his taste, and, moreover, he will be spared the
heat which towards August becomes almost
suffocating. Perhaps it is the temperature
which conduces to the idle, pleasure-seeking
mood that comes over one as soon as Baden-
Baden comes in sight. I only know that,
whereas we arrived full of good and energetic
resolutions, we quickly added ourselves to the
great majority which spends the morning in a
lazy stroll through the Forest, the afternoon
in the Kurgarten, listening to the band, and
the evening at an excellent Operetta theatre,
with a delicate supper on the verandah of the
Kurgarten restaurant. I know it is a dis-
graceful confession—I know that as professed
ramblers we should have stuck to our knapsacks and thick boots with pharisaically uplifted
noses, turned our backs on so much irresponsi-
bility, and returned to Nature's bosom. Only,
alas! (this 'alas' is wholly hypocritical, I fear)
Nature seems to be in league with the worldly
spirit which haunts Baden-Baden and leads
sturdy ramblers from the right path. Imagine
yourself, critical and disapproving reader, seated
comfortably at a table decked with flowers, a
dainty supper *à la française* before you, around

you at other similar tables a bevy of beautifully dressed women with equally elegant
cavaliers, before you the brightly lit Kurgarten,
a soft evening air perfumed with flowers brushing your face, in your ears the strains of distant
music, and straight before you, outlined against
the dying red of the evening sky, pine-covered
mountains, the stately ruins of a once mighty
castle.   And when you have succeeded in
realising the magic of this combination of
natural and artificial charms, you are at liberty
to condemn us for our idleness—if you can.
For our part, in defiance of all previous plans,
we let ourselves drift, and thanked the good
Roman Emperor Hadrian for his discovery of
the hot springs and for the subsequent building of the 'Civitas Aurelia aquensis,' as Baden-
Baden was then called.   Sharing the fate of
Badenweiler, Baden-Baden fell into neglect as
soon as the Roman Empire passed away, and
though with the building of the two castles
by the Markgrafen of Baden it recovered
something of its original importance, a final
blow delivered by the devastating armies of
the French in 1689 threatened to effectually
cut short its existence.   It is a curious irony
of fate that it is chiefly owing to the French
that Baden-Baden rose to the position of the
world's first watering-place, and though after

288

1870 the number of French visitors sank to *nil*, the tide of patriotic feeling was not strong enough to resist the temptation, and to-day the French language is heard as often as German in the streets of Baden-Baden during the high season.

It goes without saying that the municipality have done everything that was possible to add to the comfort and pleasure of the visitors. Their means were extensive, as until 1872 the gambling tables were in their hands and the returns, of course, enormous. As soon as they had collected sufficient money to arrange other distractions, they remembered that gambling is a wicked vice, and the tables were done away with, to the distress of the hotel-keepers, who believed that Baden-Baden's days were numbered. Their prophecies proved mistaken, fortunately, for, though a certain class remained away, others came, and the loss of the former was not altogether to be regretted.

In Baden-Baden boredom is banished; no matter what you are or who you are, you are sure to find something to amuse you. If you are a sportsman, there are the beautifully kept tennis courts, there is archery and fishing; if you are musical, there are excellent concerts morning, noon, and night, with the occasional appearance of some such operatic star as Caruso to break the monotony; and if merely an invalid, there are baths, springs, 'Trinkhallen' for every imaginable complaint, with every imaginable amusement to pass the 'in-between-time' agreeably. Being neither particularly fashionable nor sporting, and with no claims to the title of invalids, we felt rather like foreigners in a strange land—outsiders who, nevertheless, managed to enjoy themselves thoroughly in a shamelessly unfashionable way. And here let it be observed, for those who feel themselves frightened by fine descriptions, that Baden-Baden is by no means an expensive place, except for those who wish to make it so. It is quite true that one or two of the hotels demand prices which would make even Vienna blush; but no one is compelled to stay at them, and there are numbers of smaller places which offer comfort, if not fashion, at most reasonable rates. Nor are the amusements in the least exorbitant, though the visitor with limited means should avoid driving in the tempting-looking carriages which promenade the Lichtenthaler Allée. On account of the steep hills which surround Baden-Baden it is forbidden for a carriage to be drawn by less than two horses, and with this fact for an excuse the drivers demand equally 'steep' fares. The excuse may be justified, but it puts such extravagances out of the reach of ordinary folk, and one experience taught us that our future rambles — unless we wished to return prematurely home—would have to be performed strictly on foot.

In obedience to the law of custom, and also, perhaps, because it was the least exhausting of all the regulation 'tours,' we first turned our attention to the ruins of the Old Castle which overlooks the town. On the way upwards we passed the New Castle, so called only to distinguish it from the Old, for in reality it has no pretensions to youth. Built in 1749, it served the Markgrafen of Baden as a dwelling-place until the whole court was moved to Rastatt, and even to-day it often welcomes members of the Grand Ducal family in the quieter months of the year.

A curious story is told concerning this sudden changing of court residence. It happened that, in the year 1692, the Markgraf Ludwig Wilhelm returned in triumph from the wars in Turkey, where he had won himself both honour and treasure. Baden-Baden, then the capital of his state, decorated itself with as much magnificence as was possible, considering its ruined condition, and gave the national hero a welcome befitting his deeds and popularity. In his victorious train was a young Turkish princess, whose father had killed himself rather than yield to his conqueror, and whom the Markgraf had rescued and brought to Europe. Magnanimous and chivalrous as he was, the Markgraf did everything in his power to make the young captive's life bearable, but his wife, Sibylle, looked upon the stranger with hatred and suspicion. Her jealousy was unfounded as far as the Markgraf was concerned, but the Turkish maiden, Zoraïde, as she was named, cherished a deep love for her protector, which one day broke out in a passionate confession. The sad scene between the grave, honourably minded man and the hot-headed child — she was but fifteen years old—was overheard by the Markgrafin, whose fury amounted to madness. On her way back to her rooms the Princess Zoraïde was stabbed to death, and though it was given out that she killed herself out of home-sickness, it was noted that from that hour the Markgraf never spoke to his wife and removed his court to Rastatt. The Markgräfin took up her residence at the Castle Favorite, a few miles from Baden, and there lived an extraordinary life—six months of wild orgies were invariably followed by six months of sackcloth and ashes—but she never saw her husband again.

The 'Favorite' forms one of the most pleasant drives from Baden-Baden, and after drinking coffee under the oak trees which

surround the forester's house, the visitor would
do well to make a tour of the interesting little
castle, where he can view the scenes of the
wicked Sibylle's doings, as well as the gruesome
chapel with the horrible wax figures of the
Holy Family, at whose feet she spent her
periods of expiation.

A pleasant half-hour's walk from the New
Castle brought us to the remains of the Old,
the so-called Ruins of Hohenbaden. The way
upwards through the forest had prepared us
for an extensive view, but all expectation sank
colourless before the beauty of the outlook from
the terrace. Unfortunately a restaurant with
well-filled tables disturbed us, and with no
more than a glimpse down into the depths, we
hurried through the stone gateway and into
the peaceful precincts of the ruins, assuring
ourselves that there we should have time enough
to gaze our fill without the supercilious attentions of gentlemanly waiters, (not that the
restaurant is to be despised — certainly not.
On other occasions I have visited the Old
Castle and been graciously pleased to partake
of an excellent, if expensive, meal at one of the
white tables overlooking the valley, but on this
occasion we were feeling above such materialism
and desired poetical solitude). Taste in the
matter of ruins is very varying, and therefore

I hope to disarm all protest as regards my next remark by admitting right away that I do not count myself infallible—namely, to my mind no other ruin in the Black Forest, or even in Baden, equals that of Hohenbaden either in form or situation—and my challenge is delivered above all to Heidelberg, whose castle claims the palm. But Heidelberg Castle is a 'show' ruin, and at the bottom is just a little bit of humbug. It is too modern, too 'touched-up' to awaken any real feeling of awe. One feels a little as though one were being shown over a fine tumble-down palace of recent origin, and a visit to the renovated chapel is a final, most dreadful disillusion. But Hohenbaden is genuine. The spirit of long past centuries hovers over its roofless halls; the breeze sighing through the æolian harps seems like the voice of history telling gently and resignedly of old glorious years when fair ladies and brave knights loved and fought and died between the massive walls.

Untouched since the tragic year of 1689, when French hands brought the final ruin, it gazes proudly down on to the valley 1200 feet below, on to the town over which it once wielded sovereign sway, and seems to hold itself aloof from the irresponsible crowd of pleasure-seekers who wander carelessly about the scene of the final struggle against the hated pillagers. But indeed, to judge from the central hall, the ruins know that later history has revenged them, for there is a sunny peace over all; trees have grown up where once were stately pillars, and golden patches of sunshine alternate with cool green - tinted shadows. From the parapet which runs along the top of the wall we obtained an uninterrupted view of the valley, but, strange enough, it was still the shattered walls about us which held our attention. The quiet, the general atmosphere of drowsy content, made it seem hardly possible that a ghost should haunt the castle limits ; yet such is the case, and there are many who will testify to having seen at midnight a gray shadow pass wailing from the banqueting hall to the high tower—there to disappear. The Gray Lady, as the spectre is called, is no other than a former Markgräfin of Baden, who one' day carried her baby son to the tower of the castle and, showing him the lovely world beneath, boasted to him of the great riches and power which would one day be his. Thereupon the unhappy child struggled out of her arms and fell headlong into the abyss. The body was never found, and to-day the mother, thus heavily punished for her pride, wanders round the ruins lamenting and seeking in vain for the son she is condemned never to find. A second version of the story is that the Markgräfin had two children, and, being of a cruel, grasping disposition, she killed them, determining that the day should never come when she should have to give up her power and wealth into the younger hands. But vengeance comes sooner or later on the track of every crime, and though the wicked Markgräfin escaped earthly punishment, she was forced after death to haunt the scenes of her cruel deeds. Thus anybody who has the questionable fortune to meet the Gray Lady can choose which story pleases him best— for only one thing is certain about her, and that is that her appearance is always immediately followed by a dire misfortune to the Grand Ducal house, though it is only fair to add that the present rulers belong to another branch of the family, and are therefore only distant connections of the unhappy spirit.

From the ruins we proceeded by a somewhat steep path up to the rocks. Most wanderers miss this part of the walk because they labour under the mistaken impression that the castle marks the highest point, or because they shirk the last and rather exhausting ascent. But once the flight of stone steps have been overcome, the path is easy enough, and a quarter of an hour farther on a stone signpost points abruptly to the left. Over a wilderness of rock we at last reached the wooden bridge which leads from one giant boulder to another, and there, balanced, as it seemed to us, over the edge of a bottomless abyss, we gazed, awestruck, at the scene beneath us. I have mentioned before that actual feet and inches are of very little account in the Black Forest, where position and form, rather than height, make the grandeur of the mountains. Nowhere is this the case more than at the summit of the rocks. What is a paltry 1695 feet after the Feldberg's 4500 feet? And yet not even the Feldberg can offer a more impressive outlook, much less combine its impressiveness with a charm which is almost pastoral. Indeed, I know no other view in the Black Forest which at once arouses so deep a sense of peace, so profound a sense of awe. It is true that to the left, and directly opposite, high mountains prevent the eye from penetrating farther into the forest, but to the right stretches the broad Rhine Valley, and through the shimmering heat-mist the great river itself appears like a broad winding band of silver. Below, directly beneath the wanderer's feet, like a sea of olive-green, are the tops of the mighty pines which grow tenaciously on the face of the precipice; and beyond them, lower down, the little white town, a sparkling gem set in the heart of an emerald world, beckons invitingly. The eye, at first only capable of receiving one whole and lovely impression, begins to pick out details. A little to the right, at the base of the opposite mountain, a golden dome glitters in the sunlight. It is the Russian chapel, built by the Prince Michael Stourdza as a memorial to his son, and well worth a visit when the rambler has ten minutes to spare from the attractions of the Kurgarten. Towards the south-east the Fremersberg begins the chain of mountains which shut off Baden-Baden on three sides from the world. An hour and a half's walk from the Russian chapel brings the traveller to the unfailing tower at the summit (1578 feet), and, should he travel westwards, he will find a lonely villa, once a Franciscan monastery, to which the equally unfailing legend is attached.

A certain Markgraf, Jacob of Baden, was a great hunter as well as a pious, God-fearing man, and one night, having lost himself in the depths of the Fremersberg forest, he was overtaken by a terrific storm. In his despair he called upon God to save him, and immediately the thunder subsided, and in the sudden silence he heard the tinkling of a bell. ,Revived by hope, he guided his terrified horse in the direction from whence the sound came, and soon found himself at the door of a miserable hut. In response to a blast on his huntsman's horn, two old hermits made their appearance and offered him the rough shelter of their home. The Markgraf accepted gratefully, and the next morning, refreshed and strengthened, he was able to regain the road back to his capital. At parting he promised his humble hosts a substantial reward for their timely service, and though they probably had small confidence in the keeping of that promise, they were agreeably surprised. Markgraf Jacob proved as good as his word, for soon afterwards builders appeared on the mountain-side, and before the year was out a small monastery replaced the miserable hut in which he had taken refuge.

More wonderful and more tragic are the stories told of the Yburg, the mountain which lies to the south-west of the Fremersberg, and whose noble, though ruined, castle fascinates the idlest Baden-Badener into undertaking the necessary two and a half hours' walk. The first of the legends is illustrated by the paintings which are to be found on the walls of the Trinkhalle's covered promenade, and concerns a certain Burkhard Keller von Yburg, a young knight in the service of a dowager Markgräfin who had taken up her residence in the castle of Hohenbaden. It may be that Burkhard found the widow's court somewhat dreary, for he soon sought consolation in the company of a fair young girl from the neighbouring village of Eberstein. To visit his secret bride he was compelled to leave the castle by stealth, and it often happened that midnight struck e'er he returned to his own apartments. One night, at the cross-roads leading from Hohenbaden to Eberstein, a strange apparition appeared before him — a woman draped in white rose out of the ground and beckoned him with such wondrous magic that, though her face was hidden, the young Burkhard felt for the first time that he was in the toils of a great passion ; but before a word could pass his lips the figure vanished, and he was left alone in darkness and restless despair. The village maiden saw him no more, but every night he disappeared from the castle, only to return at dawn, a haggard, wild-eyed spectre of his former self. A page, more daring than the rest, ventured to follow him on one of these ghostly wanderings, and there, at the cross-roads, he too beheld the mysterious woman. This time the veil was thrown back, revealing a face of such noble, yet sorrowful, beauty that Burkhard, unconscious of all else, flung himself on his knees before her, uttering words of wild, incoherent love such as surely human lips had never uttered before. The hidden page saw how her white arms enfolded him and how their lips met; then, overcome by a nameless terror, he turned and fled back to the castle. The next morning the young knight was found dead, and his uncle, obeying some blind instinct, excavated the spot on which he had lain, and there found, a few feet beneath the earth's surface, the marble bust of a beautiful woman. The Roman inscription revealed that the place had once been dedicated to heathen worship, and that the marble bust was of no less a deity than Venus herself. With his own hand Burkhard's uncle destroyed the fatal image, and, to ban the evil spirits for ever, he erected a cross and stone bearing his nephew's name, which stand to this day. The body of the misguided young knight was carried over to the family vault in the castle of Yburg. Soon afterwards the family found its last representative in a drinking and gambling ne'er-do-weel, who reduced the castle to ruin and disrepute. One wild and stormy night, as the Yburg's riotous lord sat vainly contriving schemes to save himself from the difficulties in which he had become entangled, a loud knocking was heard at the courtyard door. His servants had long before fled from the scenes of his wickedness, and he was therefore compelled to answer the summons himself. A handsomely dressed stranger, bearing a goblet of wonderful red wine, immediately stepped across the threshold and begged shelter for the night in return for the goblet and its contents.

"You are welcome, stranger," was the lord's greedy answer. "I would welcome the devil himself were he the bearer of such a gift."

The two sat together carousing deep into the night, but, whereas the unknown guest retained his wits, his host rapidly succumbed to the fragrant but strangely powerful wine, and in an intoxicated state he poured out the story of his desperate straits and sought his companion's advice. Instantly a flash of cruel satisfaction passed over the other's dark face.

"Have you never thought to seek amongst the bones of your ancestors which lie in the vault beneath?" he suggested. "I have heard that great treasures lie hidden there."

Excited as he was, the lord at first shrank from the horrible proposal, but a glass more of the mysterious wine weakened his powers of resistance, and, guided by his guest, he began the descent into the cold and gloomy vaults beneath. There a kind of madness came over him. With frantic, sacrilegious hands he tore open the crumbling coffins, seeking amidst the bones of his ancestors for the supposed riches, and in his blindness he did not even spare the resting-

place of his own child. Instantly a blinding
flash of light passed through the vault, and the
Lord of Yburg, dazzled but sober, saw that his
guest had vanished, and that in his stead stood
the devil himself, stretching out bony, greedy
fingers towards his prize with the words—

"Let go your hold!"

The terrified lord staggered back from the
child's coffin and prepared himself for the ever-
lasting perdition which threatened ; but no doubt
there must have been some good in him, for at
the same moment that his satanic majesty was
about to seize upon him, a child's voice echoed
through the vault—

"Let go your hold!"

A terrific clap of thunder followed, vault
and castle crumbled together, and the Herr von
Yburg, miraculously saved from death and
damnation, set out from the ruins on a pilgrimage which was to mark the beginning of a better
life. The proof of this legend is to be found in
the second tower, which shows signs of having
been struck by a flash of lightning; but un-
believers have ventured to trace the general ruin
to the Thirty Years' War, and, later still, to the
French pillagers of 1689.

Still farther east the eye encounters the topmost ridge of the Hornisgrinde, and, closer at
hand, the Steinberg and Ruhberg. Then directly

to the left of the rocks is the 'Merkur' (the Mountain of Mercury), so called because of the god's statue which was found buried on its summit; and with this tower-crowned mountain the view from the rocks ends.

The 'Felsenmeer' (Sea of Rocks) still remains to be inspected, and for our part we lingered willingly amidst the wild, fantastically shaped boulders, between which a rough path has been cut down to the valley. Wonderful indeed are the pines and firs which in this stony, unfruitful world have managed to take root. Where their roots spring from it is hard to tell; they seem to cling by some magic strength to the face of the rock, defying the tempests which break over their proud heads, and only here and there a seared trunk tells of the enemy's lightning stroke.

Turning back from the 'Felsenmeer' we wandered north-east by a pleasantly winding path to the little village of Ebersteinburg, which lies sheltered in the heart of the valley; and still upheld by our returning energy, though with more kindly feelings towards misplaced and un-romantic restaurants, we struck along the road which leads up to the castle, and a quarter of an hour later found us seated in the Gasthaus of the ruin, preparing ourselves for a welcome dinner. During the interval between the courses my companion, who, being a true German, knows the chief ballads of her native land off by heart, gave me the benefit of Uhland's "Graf Eberstein," whereby I learnt the legend which makes the old castle famous.

The ballad tells of the Emperor Otto's unsuccessful efforts to capture Ebersteinburg from its bold defender, the Graf Eberstein, and of his not very honourable ruse when all other means failed. At the time of the siege the Emperor gave a great feast at Speyer, and knowing the daring character of his enemy, he invited the Graf Eberstein to attend, promising him security until his return to the castle. The Count accepted, suspecting no evil, and spent a merry evening dancing with the fair ones at the Emperor's court, amongst whom the Emperor's daughter won his special regard. The liking seems to have been mutual, for in the words of the poet—

"Und als er sie schwingt nun im lustigen Reigen,
Da flustert sie leise, sie kann's nicht verschweigen
Graf Eberstein
Hute dich fein
Heut' Nacht wird dein Schlosslein gefahrdet sein."

Or, in other words, for the benefit of those whose knowledge of the German language does not allow of the enjoyment of ballads, the Emperor's daughter found the Count too attractive not to take the opportunity of a dance to whisper to him that in his absence his castle was in danger. The Count needed no second warning. With all possible haste he recrossed the Rhine and reached Ebersteinburg just in time to repulse the treacherous attack of the Emperor's troops. From that hour the knight's success was assured, for the Emperor found that he had an enemy in the camp, and an enemy not to be overcome by sword or cunning. Yielding at last to his daughter's strategy and the Count's military genius, the Emperor consented to a compromise. The castle surrendered—but only to the Emperor's daughter, who crossed the threshold as the Count's bride. Thus, all's well that ends well, and it is quite a relief to find a legend that does have 'a happy ending.'

Altogether the castle seems to have been fortunate, both in its masters and in its history, for, unlike its neighbours, it has fallen peacefully into decay without the helping hand of French invaders. To-day little remains but the donjon, from whence a fine view can be obtained over the Rhine Valley ; and soon after our settlement with our host we were on our way homeward by way of the Verbrannten Felsen (burnt rocks) and the Wolfsschlucht. From the former—a wilderness of rocks rising to about twelve hundred feet—the wanderer obtains a charming glimpse of the Murg Valley; and the Wolfsschlucht, though small, is wild and romantic enough to justify the necessary detour.

From thence back to Baden we needed an hour's steady walking—a not inconsiderable matter, considering our morning's exertions and the not very exhilarating atmosphere; but the shady and beautifully kept paths minimised the distance, and there was still another legend —this time of a purely academic character— to excite our interest. Two blocks of granite, the one bearing an inscription, the other a cross, mark the spot where once the devil and an angel delivered sermons against each other— the latter, of course, coming off in triumph. A painting of the episode is to be found on the walls of the Trinkhalle, where, indeed, all the legends of the neighbourhood have been depicted for the benefit of the 'Kurgäste' on their early morning wanderings with their glass of steaming spring water. These works of art are indeed a veritable guide for the wanderer, who, if he takes each legend and makes a point of visiting the scene in which it was played, will find that he has thoroughly 'done' the Northern Black Forest. But he will have to be a very energetic wanderer—above all, steeled against the temptations of Baden-Baden herself. He must despise worldliness in every form, and feel himself above lazy saunterings down the Lichtenthaler Allée with its fresh green gardens and stately ruinous hotels. In fact, he must be a rambler *par excellence*—would that we could lay claim to the distinction! Let it be confessed, to our shame, that our longest walk after the one already described was to the nunnery at the end of the Allée—the last of its kind, and only excepted from the general suspension of the Orders in 1803 by the fact that the foundress and many of the abbesses belonged to the Grand Ducal house and are buried in the church. The nunnery was saved from the devastating French Army in 1689 by the advice of a French general, who, having been nursed by the nuns, told them to take off the slates of the roof, thus giving the place an appearance of being deserted. The ruse was successful and the nuns were spared. To-day only twenty are allowed to inhabit the building, which was founded in response to a wish expressed by St. Bernard of Clairvaux that a nunnery of his order (Cistercian) should be built on the spot. His desire was gratified by Irmengard, the widow of the Markgraf Hermann v., ninety years after the death of the great preacher.

With this visit to one of Baden-Baden's most interesting relics of the past our energy finally collapsed. We sank back luxuriously into the *dolce far niente* which is in the very air, and our advice to travellers who wish to know Baden-Baden thoroughly and realise her full charm is —Go and do likewise.

CHAPTER XV

THE LAST RAMBLE: HERRENALB AND KARLSRUHE

It was with a double regret that after a week
in Baden-Baden we mounted our long-neglected
bicycles and slowly made our way up the steep
and winding ascent which leads to Gernsbach.
In the first place the week's idleness had rather
incapacitated us for strenuous endeavour, in the
second we knew that our journeying was nearly
at an end. Past the so-called ' Fisch-Kultur,' a
simple but much-visited restaurant, we wheeled
our machines upwards through the Forest until
we reached a point where the road once more
permitted us to mount and enjoy the fruits of
our labours in a long, luxurious ' free-wheel '
down into Gernsbach. But for these blissful
interludes our bicycles would have been no more
than an encumbrance; but he who knows the
wonders of free-wheeling down the Black Forest
roads will understand that we were prepared to
walk many miles and to push our machines up

the steepest hills for the sake of a few minutes
of exertionless movement through the fresh,
pine-laden air. And for that matter the old-
fashioned little town—I call it 'town' for fear
of giving offence — offered pleasant enough
accommodation for the rest of that day and night,
and in itself is perhaps one of the most picturesque villages—pardon—towns of the Northern
Black Forest. There are no thatched cottages
or quaintly dressed peasants, but the streets
present, none the less, a quaint aspect of age
and dreamy respectability. Especially attractive
is the view from the bridge across the Murg.
The river is fairly broad at this point, and
foaming over the slanting weir seems only to be
kept within its limits on the one side by the
raised roadway, on the other by the low, irregu-
larly built houses. Close at hand is Schloss
Eberstein (not to be confused with Alt-Eberstein
or Ebersteinburg), which in 1689 suffered the
general fate at the hands of the French, but was
renovated in 1804 by the monk Graf Friedrich.
The descendants of the Graf Eberstein, whose
story has already been related, forsook the old
castle for the new, and at least one member
of the family, Graf Wilhelm, is buried in
the Protestant church at Gernsbach. For the
rest, Gernsbach is one of the chief centres of
the timber trade in the Black Forest, and in

spite of narrow streets and tumble-down houses is peacefully prosperous and little troubled by the outside world, save when a packed motor-car from Baden-Baden clanks through on its way to Herrenalb and Wildbad.

To recover from the effects of a week in the somewhat relaxing air of Baden-Baden we had promised ourselves a few days' rest in the higher regions before returning definitely to town life, and had chosen Herrenalb for the resting-place. Thus the next day saw us *en route*, now plodding up the mountain-side, now sailing gracefully down the winding road as fast as a due regard for our bones permitted. The distance being but a matter of about six miles, we reached our destination early in the day and put up at the Hotel zum Falkenstein, a charming little hotel which by some miracle or other has managed to strike the happy medium between extravagant luxury and uncomfortable simplicity. In all gratitude I must remember the pleasant evenings in the gardens which alone separated the hotel from the fir-covered mountains, the excellent meals, daintily served at small tables on the verandahs, the general atmosphere of quiet and refinement. It had not been my original intention to make much mention of our various hotels, but sometimes so much of our pleasure has depended on the kindliness of our hosts and their

THE DWARF IN THE FRAUENALB NUNNERY.

arrangements for the comfort of their guests that it seems only fair to mention them, if only for the benefit of other ramblers.

We were now in the Wurttembergischen Black Forest, which, as has already been mentioned, is not rich in beautiful spots ; but though Herrenalb has nothing of a romantic nature to show to the traveller returning from the splendours of the south, it is none the less a place most suitable both as the end or the beginning of a prolonged tour. The height (1000 feet) warrants a fresh, pure air which prepares the constitution equally well for a descent from higher levels to the lowlands, or for an ascent into the mountains. Its valley, called the Alb, after the crystal, trout-filled stream which flows down to Karlsruhe, is one of the most charming in the Northern Black Forest, and in early autumn the fiery tints which mingle with the pine on the low mountains, the contrasting emerald green of the meadows, the unbroken peace, make it a positive paradise for the weary workers in the great towns whose close proximity seems scarcely believable. Farther down towards Karlsruhe spinning manufactories have sprung up to disfigure the landscape, but from Marxzell to Herrenalb the scenery is, of its kind, perfect. As for Herrenalb itself, it must first be explained that its name is intended to distinguish it from the nunnery,

Frauenalb, which lies a few miles farther down the valley. Both the monastery at Herrenalb and the nunnery at Frauenalb owe their origin to Graf Berthold II. of Eberstein, who seems to have suffered severely from the then fashionable complaint of 'visions.' The first vision, it is true, appeared to his great friend the Graf von Zimmern, who, following the custom of the time, lost himself in the Forest whilst stag-hunting, and was met by a mysterious figure. His spectral guide led him to a castle and showed him a scene of wild revelry, in which the knight's ancestors took the chief part. Then suddenly, amidst a crash of thunder, the castle crumbled together and nothing was seen but smoke and the thick fumes of rising sulphur.

"Listen to the groans of these souls in torment and take warning!" was the parting advice of the Graf's companion. "Their fate may be yours!"

Apparently the effect was instantaneous, for with the assistance of his friend of Eberstein, Graf von Zimmern built the nunnery of Frauenalb as an expiation for his and his ancestors' sins. But even the pious nuns seem to have been infected by the evil spirits which haunted the spot, for it is to be regretfully confessed that their conduct was far from exemplary. In the fourteenth century the Abbess Margarete von

Eberstein maintained an obstinate quarrel with
the Convention, which ended in the interference
of the Markgraf of Baden, who laid the nunnery
in ashes. It was rebuilt, but again burnt down
in 1507, and with the Reformation the morals of
the inmates seem to have gone to ruin with the
rest. At any rate the conduct of the abbess was
sufficiently bad to warrant the Markgraf's decision that the nuns should be expelled and the
nunnery secularised. But the nuns were made
of bolder stuff than was to be expected from
women of their calling. They offered determined resistance, so that a small army had to
be sent up against them, and it was only after
a fierce struggle that they surrendered. Even
then their resistance was not at an end. They
appealed to the Imperial court of justice at
Speyer, and the result was the discomfiture of
the Markgraf, who was compelled to reinstate
them. Their joy over the news of the verdict
was so great that a portrait of the mounted
messenger was made on the cloister door.
A quaint dwarf's figure is also to be found in
the garden, and commemorates the first announce-
ment that the Thirty Years' War was at an end.

But the quarrel between the nuns and their
liege lord, the Markgraf of Baden, continued.
Perhaps upheld by the fact that the nunnery
lies just over the border-line which separates

Baden from Württemberg, they attempted to obtain complete independence, and again military force had to be used to convince them of their mistake. Very shortly afterwards the Peace of Lunéville finally settled the quarrel, to the satisfaction of Baden, and the troublesome nuns were expelled for ever. The building was used for a cloth manufactory, but the sacrilege was shortly afterwards punished by a fire which laid the old nunnery in ruins, and since then they have been allowed to rest in peace.

It will be seen from this brief outline that the Graf von Zimmern's pious act seems to have been of but small avail, and for aught I know the ill-fated nunnery may still be haunted by the evil spirits which witnessed its foundation. In daylight, however, the ruins are merely picturesque and make an admirable goal for an afternoon's walk or bicycle ride (lazy folk can make use of the little electric tram which runs from Herrenalb to Karlsruhe). Coffee should be drunk in the restaurant inside the ruins, and imaginative persons should be on the look out for the entrance to the secret underground passage which connected the monastery to Frauenalb—as a means of escape in times of danger, so the guide-books say. Also there is a gloomy spot where my German friend assured me the renegade nuns were buried alive, and though I have nothing but her word for the truth of the story I give it in the hope that it may cause the reader an agreeable shudder.

But to return to Herrenalb! The monastery owed its foundation to that already mentioned Graf Berthold von Eberstein, who, in 1180, probably infected by his friend, beheld a warning vision, and as a result the Cistercian monastery was built in the following year. The place seems to have suffered even worse than the nunnery. The Reformation made the inmates turn out for the benefit of the Protestant clergy, and the Thirty Years' War reduced the building to such a state of ruin that to-day nothing remains but the old church with the tomb-stones of the family Eberstein. The little roof-less chapel bears the name of ' Paradise,' though why I do not know, unless it is because of its sunny peace. The chief curiosity of the place is the tall fir tree which grows on the top of the slender arch of the doorway, having its roots no one knows where, but successfully defying wind and lightning. The neighbour-ing church has been successfully renovated, but where the monastery once stood only a large bath establishment for the health seekers is to be found. Added to all this Herrenalb possesses a Kurgarten, and in the high season a string-band, which discourses sweet music twice daily ;

but somehow or other everything is on such a miniature scale that one is not in the least offended at the attempt. Altogether Herrenalb gives the impression of being a big plaything : the shops and bazaars are so small and dainty, the houses and villas are so brightly coloured, that it is very difficult to take them seriously, and even the Falkenstein Rocks, which overlook the valley, though reputed majestic, scarcely seem more than a finishing touch to the whole. Curiously enough Herrenalb is one of the few places in South Germany where private villas are plentiful, a fact which speaks well for its popularity. Its popularity is perhaps a little too marked in the months of July and August, but in June, even in the latter half of May, it offers a wonderful peace and fresh green loveliness to those whose time and purse does not allow of a longer journey.

After a few days' rest and refreshment we once more shouldered our knapsacks and set out on the final stages of our travels. The shortest route to our eventual destination, Karlsruhe, was by way of Frauenalb and Ettlingen (a delightful downhill ride of about twelve miles), but with the very human desire to put off the evil day we had decided on a flying visit to the great Wurttembergisch watering-place Wildbad. It is to be confessed

that the term 'flying' is a little misplaced,
for the first ascent of the Dobel mountain, which
divides Herrenalb from Wildbad, was steep in
the extreme, and the combined burdens of our
knapsacks and bicycles threatened to become
overwhelming. But after an hour's steady
climbing the open, wind-swept summit was
reached and our reward close at hand. From
thence onward the beautiful road wound down
into the valley in graceful curves, which left
us no work save that of keeping a firm hold
on the brakes, and half an hour later we were
once more on the level and wheeling our way
southwards to Wildbad. We were now in the
narrow Enz Valley, whose chief charm lies
in the pine-covered mountains which rise up
abruptly on either side. In the strict sense of
the word they are not mountains, but merely
the rocky walls of a cutting, and if the traveller
has energy enough to make the ascent he will
be surprised to find himself in a rich pasture
and meadow land bearing little resemblance
to the usual Black Forest type of scenery.
Wildbad lies in the narrow end of the valley, and
is the only important town of which the region
can boast.

In spite of a theatre, Kurgarten, Kurhaus,
and all the other adornments of a fashionable
watering-place, Wildbad has never succeeded in

approaching its rival Baden-Baden in popularity amongst the genuine pleasure-seekers. Unlike the majority of Black Forest Bader its waters are of genuine utility, and, as a consequence, Wildbad is above all else a resort of those seeking health and rest. The worldly ones keep away for the most part. The extremely closed-in situation makes the heat in summer unpleasantly oppressive, and in winter the climate is rough in proportion, so that ordinary folk needing fresh, bracing air prefer the mountains, and those on the outlook for pure pleasure pass on as a matter of course to Baden-Baden. Nevertheless, interesting rambles can be made into the Murg and Nagold valleys, and there are pleasant walks enough for guests whose energies have been reduced by the relaxing atmosphere. A funicular has even been erected in late years, so that when the heat becomes intolerable it is easy enough to escape from the valley to the cooler heights of the mountains. Fine hotels and bath establishments are perhaps the chief attractions of Wilbad, whose surroundings, though lovely enough in an unpretentious way, cannot compare with those of the Badische watering-places. With perfect right Wildbad calls itself the Queen of the Wurttembergisch Black Forest—but the Wurttembergisch Black Forest is but a small part of the whole, and I even venture to suggest that of the two Herrenalb is the more likely to win the preference of ordinary mortals not afflicted with gout and other ailments which the flesh is heir to. For our part, being sound in body, we found nothing to excuse our putting off the evil day of our return homewards, and early the next morning we were riding to our last stopping-place, Pforzheim. As the greatest jewellery manufacturing town in Germany, it may be imagined that it has but little to offer in the way of scenic attractions, and our night's rest there was made solely in order that we might be able to bicycle the next day to Karlsruhe. Nevertheless, Pforzheim has historical interest enough. As the northern gate to the Black Forest, it was once the site of a Roman Kastell, and in later generations bore a lion's share in the ruin and suffering of the French invasions. To-day the visitor's impression is one of prosperity, peace, and cleanliness. The dirt and confusion of a big manufacturing town are wholly absent; it is indeed hard to believe that 26,000 workmen are engaged in the 800 manufactories of which the town boasts!

And now our last ride is at hand, and it is not less beautiful because the Black Forest has been left behind us, and only the distant line of mountains reminds us of the land of forest and pine through which we have wandered. Our level road leads through leafy forest and wide stretches of open, prosperous land; on either hand apple and cherry trees mark our way, and there is no more lovely sight than the road from Pforzheim to Karlsruhe in the season when the fruit trees bear their blossom. Then I have seen it as a veritable fairyland, and even on this occasion there is enough pastoral loveliness to satisfy even the spoilt Black Forest wanderer accustomed to Dame Nature's grandest effects. And, apart from the scenery, there are the quaint South German villages, with their low white cottages, their healthy barefooted children, their storks' nests, their pleasant inns and friendly inhabitants. The traveller who has accompanied us so far would do well to follow our last example and take his midday meal at the sunny village of Berghausen, where mine host of the Gasthaus zum Laub will give him a courtly welcome in the old oak-lined parlour, show him, in between the courses, paintings presented him by famous painters who have visited the place, and last, but by no means least, the tame stork who, on account of a broken wing, condescends to spend the rough winter under German skies, when a curious-looking pair of red stockings help him to resist the cold. And so onward through the peaceful country until the old Roman tower of Durlach rises to the left, warning us that our destination is close at hand.

Once the capital of Baden, Durlach has sunk to little more than a rather dirty suburb of Karlsruhe, and bears scarcely a trace of its ancient origin and troubled history. Only the tower on the hill tells of the first Roman soldiery who, from that vantage-ground, kept watch over the Rhine Valley. A couple of miles farther along the broad, straight high-road and we have already crossed the boundary of the modern capital, Karlsruhe, and, dusty and travel-worn, ride down the chief street, proudly conscious of the deeds of prowess which lie behind us.

Karlsruhe—Karl's rest—owes its name to the founder, who, having quarrelled with his Parliament at Durlach, removed his residence to the present site in the hopes that in the idyllic seclusion of the forest he might find peace. That his subjects found they could not live without him is a fact which is not to be regretted by the present generation, for Karlsruhe, though still peaceful, is one of the most pleasant 'Residenzen' of South Germany; and whether it be chosen as a starting-point for the Black Forest or as a resting-place before undertaking the homeward journey to England, a short stay can be made very agreeable. Even rambles are still to be indulged in, and if the visitor is a wise man, he will request his hotel porter to procure him a day's card for the Wildpark, and then lose himself, either on foot or on bicycle, in the lovely *allées* of oak and beech. Or if he be desirous of reaching some goal, let him choose the Freidrich's Allée and, having passed the cross-roads of the forester's little hut, take the first turning to the left and pass through the gates and over the railway to the Grand Duke's hunting-box at Stutensee, where a pleasant forester's house will provide him with shelter and refreshment. The hour and a half's ride is as lonely as it is beautiful, and the rambler must expect to meet no one but an occasional forester, who may ask him for his card, and perhaps a herd of deer—or boars. The latter, be it mentioned, are quite harmless.

But all this region belongs to the Hardtwald, not to the Black Forest; and so, with Karlsruhe for our last stopping-place, we close our rambles. True, they have not exhausted the Black Forest —many will say we have but skirted the inner beauties of the country—but at least those who have followed us will have seen some of the chief, as well as the most secluded, spots. They will have twice crossed the full breadth of the forest, from west to east and from east to west, and will have passed over the highest regions of the north, haphazard, it is true, using every means of locomotion that presented itself, but still gaining a deeper glimpse into the real characters of the country and its people than can be obtained by those who cling vigorously to plans and time-tables. And if this little book, written by one Black Forest lover to other Black Forest lovers, and, above all, to those to whom the name conveys no feeling and no meaning, has opened the gates a little wider to a country which, in its character, its unfathomable spirit, has no rival, it has served its purpose and needs, therefore, no apology.

Printed by
MORRISON & GIBB LIMITED
Edinburgh

Lightning Source UK Ltd.
Milton Keynes UK
UKHW010956030323
417983UK00006B/374